HAND ANALYSIS

*A Technique for Knowl-
edge of Self and Others*

HAND ANALYSIS

A TECHNIQUE FOR KNOWLEDGE OF SELF AND OTHERS

Myrah Lawrance

PARKER PUBLISHING COMPANY, INC.

West Nyack, N.Y.

PRINTED IN THE UNITED STATES OF AMERICA

B & P

This book is lovingly dedicated to the memory of my late husband, H. Walker Lawrance. His knowledge, understanding, and help made it possible.

WHAT PALMISTRY CAN REVEAL

"Experience is the best teacher" may be an old adage, but it is as true today as it was when it was first coined. We have applied this axiom to our study of Hand Analysis. In our years of practical experience in this field, we have analyzed over 200,000 hands. Our experience has been both extensive and highly varied, since we have analyzed hands belonging to individuals from every walk of life.

In this book, we will give you the benefit of our vast experience. We will show you how, by careful study of this material, you, too, will be able to learn to analyze hands scientifically.

You will be told the truth about Hand Analysis, and you will be told about the fallacies preached by many incompetents. We will show you what Hand Analysis can reveal, and we will also show you what it cannot reveal.

Do you have talent for music, art, or any of the creative arts? You will find the answer in your own hands.

Are you aware that your disposition and temper are reflected in your hands? And that your Love Life is no secret to anyone who can read the map of your hands?

Did you know that a woman's hand will reflect the work of her husband? It certainly will. Especially if she is very dependent on him.

Does your hand show the exact number of children in your family? Yes, not necessarily the number in your immediate family, but the children touching your life in some way.

Does travel, either foreign or domestic, reveal itself in your hand? Or, perhaps, a change of location? The answer is Yes.

Do hands indicate what type of vocation would be best suited for you? Definitely.

The hand, however, is *not* the prognosticator of illness to come. Nor will it foretell of sudden death by an accident, or by suicide. There is, however, one exception to this rule. Violent fever in early childhood always leaves a definite mark upon the hand. This will be discussed later in this book.

Will you remain active throughout the years of your life? Or will you put yourself on the shelf at an early age, and sit around waiting to die?

Will you have friends and security in your old age? Or will you be dependent on charity and live a lonely existence?

The answers to these questions can all be found in your own hands. A careful study of all the information we will give you in this book, will enable you to find the answers in the lines on the palms of your hands.

All the important facts connected with the Hand, are illustrated by the use of photographs, line drawings, and imprints of actual hands.

Although we have Hand Prints of many famous people, we have purposely omitted most of them. Instead, we have included photographs of "Hands at Work" and we will show you why these hands are particularly suited for the job they are doing.

We dedicate this book to you, the reader, with the hope that you will discover truths about yourself that will make your life happier and more interesting both to you and your loved ones.

LEARNING TO BECOME
A HAND ANALYST

Hand Analysis is a science. It cannot be called one of the exact sciences, like mathematics, where two plus two always make four. Or chemistry where two parts of hydrogen and one part oxygen will make water.

In an exact science, we are dealing with certain, fixed and unchangeable facts. In Hand Analysis we are dealing with a human being—an uncertain equation, since no two humans are ever exactly alike. However, certain indications of the same general type will show certain similar attributes.

Webster defines Palmistry as: "The *pretended* art of foretelling the future by examination of the lines and marks in a person's hand." We hereby heartily agree with Mr. Webster. We do *not* believe that *anyone's exact future can be foretold accurately by any means whatever.* Any man or woman who claims to be able to do so, is a charlatan and a fraud.

We do say, however, that Hand Analysis can reveal the general outline of the potential of the individual's future. In other words, an accurate Hand Analysis will point toward the general direction in which an individual should go in order to get the most out of his life. A study of thousands of hands of old people clearly proved that they did not follow the blueprint indicated in their hands and therefore failed to get all the good they would have gotten had they heeded the "message" in the palms of their hands.

To the expert, all hands show indisputable facts. They show general temperament, character, emotional nature, kindliness or coldness. They also show vocational possibilities. In fact, the entire gamut of human weaknesses and strengths can be read in a person's hands. These same hands are also mirrors of past events—those happenings in a person's life which have had a great influence upon him.

"Upon what do we base our Science of Hand Analysis?" The answer to that question is self-evident. Hand Analysis, like any other science, is arrived at by observation, elimination, action, reaction and the study of cause and effect.

If a dozen hands showed like tendencies, it could be called coincidence. But when a thousand, ten thousand, a hundred thousand hands of the same general pattern and markings show the same characteristics, then there is definite evidence that there is direct correlation existing. Many people who take up the study of Hand Analysis, either for entertainment or to practice it professionally, make the mistake of not going into the subject thoroughly. They do not want to take the time and put in the effort necessary to master the fundamentals of Hand Analysis. This is a *must*, however, if you do not want to entirely miss some of the most important things which you should know before you can have a complete understanding of the Story of the Hands.

Unfortunately, the average person interested in Hand Analysis wants to begin at the top—namely with the lines of the hand. This, of course, is entirely the wrong approach. You would not expect to learn to play a sonata at your first piano lesson. You would know that you'd have to learn the scale and the relative position of each note in that scale before you could even attempt to play a composition of that kind. You would instinctively realize that unless you first acquired a fundamental knowledge of music, you could never even hope to become skillful enough to play that sonata.

The same reasoning holds true in Hand Analysis. If you want

to become proficient in this field, you will have to follow a definite fixed course of study. Before you can begin to analyze the lines of the hands, you must have a thorough knowledge of these three things: 1. The Hand; 2. The Thumb; 3. The Fingers.

You will find this book an excellent guide in learning the various steps to be followed in order to become an expert Hand Analyst. If you will proceed slowly and carefully, noting everything of interest as you go along, you will eventually be able to give a complete and accurate Hand Analysis—whether for entertainment purposes, or as a professional.

We have divided this book into 14 chapters. The titles will give you a clue to the principal divisions of Hand Analysis.

We cannot impress upon you too strongly the importance of taking every detail of the hand into consideration when analyzing it.

You cannot take one outstanding characteristic of a hand and definitely place the person possessing it into a specific classification. Other indications shown on the entire hand may completely change what at first appeared to be predominant.

Analysis of hands would be simple if all were of a definite type. This is not the case, however. All hands differ in many aspects. Hands are very complex, and each one shows contradictions. You have to learn, through practice and study, to fit these contradictions into a certain pattern. It is the complexity of hands that makes the science of their analysis so fascinating, and repays you for the time and effort you put into the mastery of their intricacies.

And now we would like to give some special advice to those who are seriously considering becoming Practitioners in the art of Hand Analysis.

Many will look upon you as a "fortune teller," and as such you will be expected to be able to make all sorts of predictions. The average person simply does not understand the *true* purpose of Scientific Hand Analysis.

It is up to you, the Practitioner, to educate those with whom you come in contact. Be frank in your analysis, but tell only what you see. Do *not* draw upon your imagination. The facts in the hand—the lines—tell the story. You have no need to fictionalize. And do not try to crowd in too many things. It is much better to pick out a half dozen salient features (dwell upon these and explain them thoroughly) than it is to skim over too many points and say nothing really constructive. Always put your clients at ease. Let them understand immediately that you are no miracle worker and that you cannot say the magic words that will dispel all their troubles.

Since they have come to you for help, however, you are entitled to ask a reasonable number of questions in order to establish certain facts, just as a doctor or a lawyer is allowed to ask questions.

Then, there are always those who will heckle you. Do *not* permit this. Be positive of your facts, and then state them positively. This will inspire confidence in you.

Stay away from morbid or depressing things. Yet, you should

point out frankly and fairly, but pleasantly, the difficulties to be overcome as seen in the hand. But do not predict death, separation, divorce or other tragedies. In the first place you *cannot* do so with accuracy. In the second place you *should not*.

Do not state anything in the presence of others which might embarrass your client. Try to be of help to every person whose hand you read.

Use constructive psychology. Strengthen weak points, and do not discourage anyone. In short, use great care in expressing yourself.

"Am I capable of becoming a good Hand Analyst?" you ask. The answer, of course, depends on you, yourself. The more you study, the more you practice, the more intelligence and patience you have, the more tact and diplomacy you possess, the further you will go in this field. The greater your knowledge of life and the more you know about people, the more proficient you will become in this Science. In short, those of you who possess an alert mind and are good reasoners, should become competent practitioners.

When you actually start analyzing hands, do *not* pose as an expert. Be fair. Say that you are just a beginner. To gain experience, check and recheck as many hands as possible. Practice on your friends and people whom you know well. In that way, you will be able to check whether your analysis fits in with the known facts.

Always remember that "A little learning is a dangerous thing." Therefore, be sure to obtain as much "learning" as possible before you consider yourself a Hand Analyst. For this Science deals with the most personal and intimate details of an individual's life, and therefore should be treated with awe and respect both by the client and the Analyst.

CONTENTS

HAND ANALYSIS

A Technique for Knowledge of Self and Others

1

THE HAND

The entire hand—fingers, thumb and palm taken collectively —is the first consideration in your search for its interesting revelations. From its color, texture, size, shape and consistency, you get your first insight into the general characteristics of its owner.

In the inspection of a hand, note its characteristics in this order:

1. Shape. 2. Size. 3. Texture. 4. Consistency. 5. Color.

Since it is necessary to start at the beginning in order to "build up a case" against the hand, we will begin with:

The Shape

Hands, for the sake of easy classification, can be placed into six different types, or shapes. They are:

1. The Primitive or Savage Hand.
2. The Square or Materialistic Hand.
3. The Spatulate or Useful Hand.
4. The Conic or Creative Hand.
5. The Psychic or Spiritual Hand.
6. The Knotty or Scholarly Hand.

Each shape, or type of hand, has a certain and definite meaning. Therefore, you must be able to recognize quickly the distinguishing features of a hand which will catalog it for you into the nearest classification.

It is seldom, if ever, that you will find any hand that is distinctly pure of type or shape. This is explained in the chapter on Mixed or Combination Hand. However, there is usually some outstanding feature of every hand that will put it into one of the seven classifications.

The Primitive or Savage Hand

You may never find the pure primitive, or savage hand. The possessors of such hands have so little interest in anything that transcends the purely material that they are unlikely to be attracted to the uplifting and helpful science of Hand Analysis. The Primitive Hand, however, is so revealing in its type, that it must be taken into consideration.

This hand is coarse and hard. The palm is large and heavy at its base. The fingers are usually short, broad and thick. They seldom possess any distinct tip. The thumb is, as a rule, not large but set low and very coarse. Most generally it is rigid, and occasionally it will be found supple in the first joint. If this is so, the owner will be the sort who throws money away on gross pleasures for himself, but is selfish where others are concerned. If the thumb has a short, thick first joint and a sort of bump on the cushion part of this joint, your subject has a furious and unpleasant nature. This animalistic brutality will come to the surface on the slightest provocation.

The Primitive Hand is usually reddish in color, coarse in texture and has the minimum of lines upon its palm. The mounts or bumps under the fingers are usually lacking. This shape or type of hand is far more prevalent in men than in women, but it may appear in either sex and has the same general meaning.

The Square or Materialistic Hand

This is the most common of all shapes and types of hands (Fig. 1-1). It is easily recognized by the apparent squareness of the palm. The fingers, being of the same relative length, give the

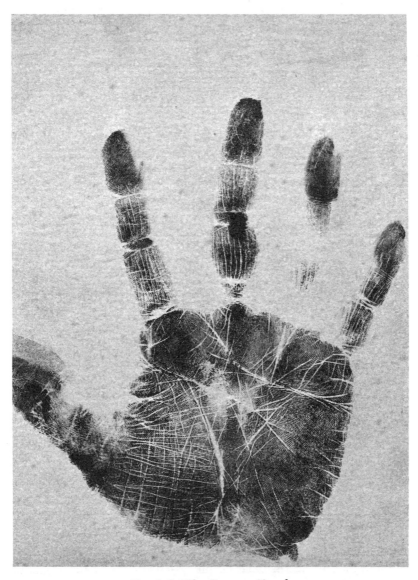

Fig. 1-1. The Square Hand.

entire hand a blunt, broad aspect. The nails are usually broad on the tips and seldom taper toward the base. The ends of the fingers are either rounded or squarish in shape. The thumb, however, is usually set rather high, showing good mentality and reasoning power.

The outstanding significance of the Square Hand is Practicability. The man or woman with the pure type of square hand is orderly in all things. The square handed person dislikes confusion, and he is not gullible. He wants facts, not theories. He is a better executive than a creator. The Square Hand belongs to a person who is usually determined, but not necessarily stubborn. He is usually just and fair in all things. The person possessing a Square Hand could do well in medicine, dentistry, law, science or business.

Figure 1-2 is an outstanding example of the Square Hand. Note particularly the finger tips. These are typical of men in the medical profession. You will notice that the finger tips are almost blunt, indicating a good mechanic in his particular work. The absence of lines is another good indication. He is thorough, steady and sympathetic in his approach.

The Spatulate or Useful Hand

The distinguishing mark of this shape of hand is the ends of the fingers. These appear to be flattened out and are somewhat wider at the end than at the first joint. The palm is square. The thumb is fairly long and has the same appearance at the end as do the fingers. The fingers are usually of average length, or a trifle longer, and are mostly smooth and straight. The hand has a good color and generally possesses well defined, strong lines. The texture is good; neither too fine nor too coarse.

The Spatulate Hand is that of a person who can work well with his hands. We have found that, contrary to the general opinion that musicians have pointed, delicate finger tips, most of them possess the Spatulate type of hand. This type is also found belonging to the highly skilled mechanic and to many surgeons.

The outstanding characteristic of the Spatulate Hand is origi-

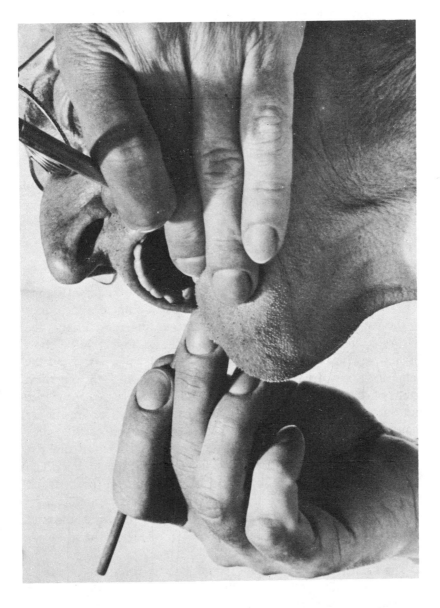

Fig. 1-2.

nality of thought and independence of action. It is the hand of energy and industry. It is the type of hand that not only likes to conceive ideas, but executes them as well.

Figure 1-3 is a perfect example of the Spatulate Hand. It is the hand of a skilled mechanic.

Notice the absence of lines in this hand. Only the Four Major lines are present. These are, the Life Line, the Fate Line, the Head Line and the Heart Line. Here these lines are very clear and deep cut, which indicates quickness of thought and the ability to act in emergencies. Because this man works with heavy, powerful machinery, this fact is quite an asset in his work.

Study this hand very carefully. You will encounter many like it in your analysis.

The Conic or Creative Hand

This hand is easily detected by the set of the fingers (Fig. 1-4). These appear to slope inward, bringing a pointed appearance to the whole hand at the end of the second finger. As a rule, the first and third fingers are of equal length and appear to be short in comparison to the second finger. The little finger is about the same length as the combined distances of the second and third joints of the third finger. The palm is rather square in appearance but has a very wide outswing on the inside edge. The fingers are generally smooth and straight, with the exception of the index and little finger. These have a tendency to curve inward slightly. The color is good and the texture is medium fine to fine. The thumb is mostly high set, long and flexible, both in the first and second joint. The fingers are nearly always supple and can be bent back sharply at the joining of the palm. The first joints at the fingers nearly always turn backward when the hand is extended to its full length.

The Creative or Conic Hand is the Artistic Hand, or at least it gives appreciation of artistic things. Persons with this type of hand are mostly swayed by impulse and first impressions. If the hand possesses few lines, it is wise for these people to follow their first impressions. If the hand is crisscrossed by many fine lines, it

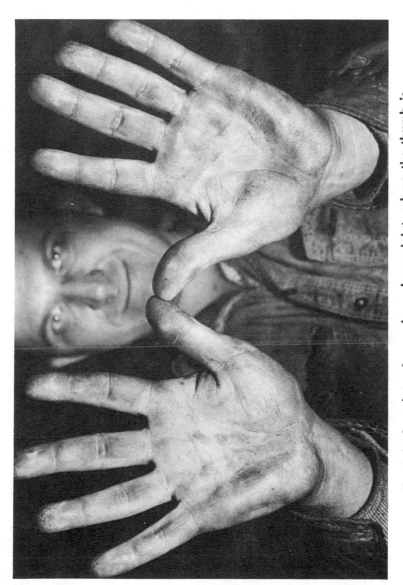

Fig. 1-3. Spatulate. A very large lower joint, where the thumb is joined to the hand, marks the individual with uncanny ability to persuade others to his way of thinking.

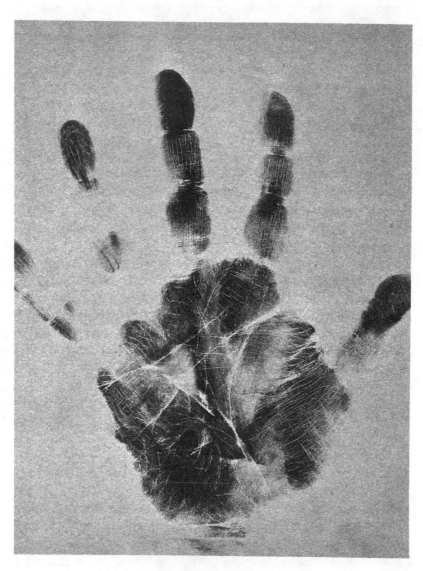

Fig. 1-4. Imprint of a creative hand.

is not wise to let their impulses govern them too much. These individuals are restless. They cannot stand monotony. They must keep busy with a variety of things. They are usually quick in thought and impulsive in speech. Their tempers flare quickly, but they also get over their anger very quickly. Since they are likeable and friendly, they are often imposed upon because of their lack of discernment of things under the surface.

The Creative or Conic Hand belongs to the creator of intellectual things. Imagination is one of the main assets of these individuals. If the hand is firm and strong, with a good will indicated by a strong thumb, its owner will get along very well in the world. If the hand is soft and flabby with a weak thumb, there will be so much shifting of ideas, actions and thoughts that the possessor will find the old saying about the "rolling stone gathering no moss" only too true.

Figure 1-5 is an excellent illustration of the true Conic or Creative Hand. These hands belong to a successful Washington, D.C. artist. There is a decided peculiarity in the photograph of these hands. Do you see it? The artist paints with his left hand.

Notice the wide flare between the second and third fingers. The same applies to his second and first fingers. This indicates originality of thought and action. (This artist's work is decidedly original, both in execution and color.)

The wide outswing on the outer edge of the palm is clearly shown, giving him intuitive imagination. His long smooth fingers show inspirational ability. His is the soul of a dreamer. The round finger tips and long firm thumb, however, reveal the ability to make dreams become actuality on canvas.

The Spiritual or Psychic Hand

This type of hand is the most beautiful and pleasing of all hands, but it is not a practical one. You will probably seldom come in contact with the pure Spiritual Hand. It is rather fortunate that there are few of these. You will recognize this hand by its slender length, its smooth, pointed fingers and its paleness, which sometimes goes to dead white. The texture is

Fig. 1-5. Creative Hand. Long thumbs, usually quite rigid, portray a "fussy" person. Such persons are exacting bosses. They insist on perfection but do not have patience to do routine work.

mostly very fine, with skin so thin that the veins show through in a bluish tint. The hand is fragile in its beauty and just as helpless as it is beautiful. The Psychic or Spiritual Hand should only belong to the person who will never have to worry about the necessities of life. Those who possess this hand are too visionary and idealistic for our modern, competitive world.

Beauty in every form appeals to the possessor of this hand. Artistic talents are usually predominant, but if these express themselves, it is usually on a basis of "art for art's sake," rather than in a desire for material reward.

These individuals are usually high-strung, and are of a decidedly nervous type. They are sensitive to an extreme, and are always imagining slights and hurts. Women possessing such hands generally desire marriage to avoid the responsibilities of supporting themselves. Men who belong in this category often resort to tricky schemes to obtain the necessities and luxuries of life.

The Knotty or Scholarly Hand

The distinguishing feature of this hand is the large joints. The fingers do not set tightly together because of these joints. As a result, light always shows between them.

The palm is mostly square at the bottom, but inclined to be long, as are the fingers. The thumb sets high. It is flexible, with a long, strong first joint and a rather "waisted" appearing second joint, which is also long. The nails are either broad and short, or broad and long.

This unusual type of hand belongs to the thinker. The owner of such hands is kind hearted, and will prove to be an excellent, faithful friend. Tact and diplomacy are his strong points, but originality of ideas is his predominant characteristic.

Sincerity and good judgment are shown in these hands. Imagination and vision are also present, but these will always flow in practical channels. Friendliness is found in the Knotty Hand. It is a type of friendliness that brings many acquaintances, but, through choice, very few really close friends.

The possessor of the Scholarly Hand will not be driven by the opinion of others. He will consider all sides of a question when it is presented, and then make his own decision according to the dictates of both his mind and conscience.

If the fingers of the Scholarly Hand have unusually large joints (as to appear almost deformed), you may have a person with a radical turn of mind; but even in their radicalism, these persons will adhere to certain high ideals and ideas.

The Scholarly Hand is that of the Inventor, the Historian, the Professor, the Judge, the Statesman, the Minister and the Reformer. (See Figure 1-6.)

The hand is firm, but not hard. The lines are many and deeply cut. The Life Line unusually long. The Head Line, with a pointed fourth finger, shows good judgment, tact, diplomacy and conversational ability. The branching formation on the Head Line shows clear thinking and expression of thought, action and organizing ability. The Financial Line is progressive, indicating success, both financially and otherwise, in more than one field of endeavor. The lines beneath the third finger show love of people and fondness of the arts and society.

The Size of the Hand

The size of the hand should be proportionate to the rest of the body. If the body is large, the hand should be large, or the reverse. Any deviation will sometimes have a marked bearing upon the story of the hand.

A large hand is in reality the best hand. A large hand is a capable hand. It usually belongs to the man or woman who is energetic and healthy. Large hands are, as a rule, of good color and usually have a certain heaviness of texture.

Small hands are the hands of individuals who like little things. The small handed person is very particular, even "finicky" at times. He or she is a stickler for detail. You will find this trait pronounced in more ways than one. The person with a small hand will not only have a lot of patience in doing things which require the most careful attention to detail, but will also go into the minutest detail in telling of any incident or happening.

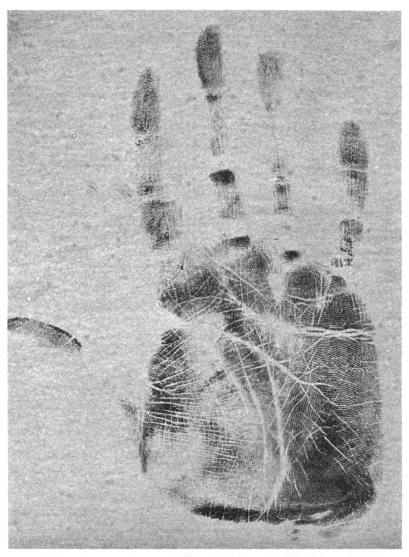

Fig. 1-6. Knotty or Scholarly Hand.

The large hand is just the opposite. It wants to do things in a big way. It cannot be bothered with little, worrisome trifles. It grasps big things and does them in a big way.

The large hand is the hand of the doer . . . the small hand that of the dreamer. Men with large hands excel in business, or any practical pursuits. Women with large hands usually possess a great deal of organizing and executive ability.

If the hands are entirely out of balance with the rest of the body, then some of the essential characteristics are overthrown. For example, an extraordinarily large hand attached to a pair of slender wrists that are not muscular, indicates a driving force of will that the physical body cannot match. On the other hand, hands too small for the rest of the body will show traces of indolence and a desire on the part of the owner to want to plan things but not to execute them. The possessors of such hands usually operate on the premise of "let George do it."

Very thick, large hands are always those of a person whose animal emotions are highly developed. Couple this sort of hand with heaviness of texture and floridity of color and you have an individual who is very gross in his sensibilities, but nevertheless possesses a great deal of physical energy. If he will direct this energy into the right channels he will make a success of his life along his own chosen pathway. Misdirect it, and he is liable to become, a failure, the pawn of his own passions.

Very thin, small hands are those of the extremely restless, nervous, irritable person. If these hands are pale or white in color, there is little stability in the person's temperamental or spiritual makeup.

Large thin hands are those of the person who possesses unbounded nervous energy and brain power. This type of hand is very often associated with those of rather unconventional ideas. If the fingers are unusually long, the hand is decidedly artistic or creative. Its owner usually has great ability to express himself clearly on any subject with which he is familiar.

Small, plump hands are those of indolence and ease. Persons possessing such hands can work hard if they are forced to do so, but they will usually try to take shortcuts to avoid anything that may be too strenuous. If these hands are unusually pinkish or reddish, it signifies strong emotions that are often hard to control. This particular type of hand denotes an avaricious nature, always trying to get something for nothing.

In these examples we have given you the extreme in every case. Fortunately in hand analysis we do not often find the extremes. However, from these you can ground yourself in the significance of each type and thereby formulate your opinions on the modified classifications you will contact in your practical analysis of actual hands. This method of remembering what the extremes mean is excellent for establishing in your mind various points from which to work when contacting modified cases.

Texture of the Hands

The next step in the understanding of the story of the hand, is its texture . . . that is the "feel" and appearance of the skin. Texture plays an important part in nature. The coarser things, whether these be animal or plant, are the hardier and stronger.

So it is with humans. The coarseness, or fineness of people can be detected in many ways. The features, the hair, the entire bone structure, the skin, the feet and the hands all tell their individual and collective tales. But as the hands are our interest, we will devote our analysis to them.

After having cataloged the hand by its color, next consider the texture. This is best done by examining the skin on the back of the hands, or even on the wrists, because hard work or lack of proper care of the hands will often coarsen the palm. In your examination note this: Is the skin unusually coarse, with large pores and having a "rough" feel? If so, you have "heavy texture." This type of skin will generally belong to a person possessing much physical strength and vitality. It also denotes animal magnetism and strong materialistic inclinations. "Heavy Texture" is mostly associated with large "reddish or brownish" hands. Occasionally you will find it with lighter colored hands, too. In such cases the trend of influence is to "coarsen" the finer qualities indicated. For example, very pale hands with a smooth, fine skin would denote extreme sensitiveness and reserve almost to the point of timidity. "Heavy texture" of the skin would make the temperament rather pugnacious in a petty way. This sort of hand would not belong to the "open fighter" type, but rather to one who would be quarrelsome and faultfinding, with a tendency to use underhanded methods to gain a point or to obtain revenge. Whenever coarseness appears in the texture of the skin in hands which do not have "coarse" color, you may be assured that a certain amount of "hardness" is injected into that particular nature which the hand heralds.

On the reverse, hands having a "heavy texture" coloring, but fineness of texture, will tell you there is a softening influence somewhere in that person which counteracts the apparent story of the color.

To illustrate: You may encounter a hand belonging to a hard driving businessman. Everything about his hand will denote his ambition, his energy and his keenness of mind. However, the texture of his skin may be quite fine. If so, his interests may lie in a business where he is dealing with fine things, such as jewelry, silks, etc. Furthermore, under his apparent "hard" exterior he may be extremely considerate of others.

Another illustration: Here is the hand of a true artist, musician, writer, or painter. His hand, in every detail, speaks loudly of his talent. But the skin is extremely coarse and seemingly out of place with every other characteristic in his hand. In this case the artist may delight in crashing, thundering music, if that is his line; or the painting of pictures, wild in color and execution, or in the writing of stories bristling with action.

Rarely, though, do you find decided extremes between coloring and texture. These two essentials seem to go very much together. However, when you contact a marked difference be careful to get the variances definitely dovetailed before proceeding further in your analysis.

You will be helped to determine a variance between coloring and texture by this fact that is worth remembering. The contrast will be so great that you will recognize it at once. Do not try to draw too fine a line of demarkation. To all practical purposes, unusualities are enough to consider. When these appear do not overlook them. To do so is to lose an important link in your chain of "evidence."

By the time you have examined 50 to 100 hands, you should be able to tell at a glance whether or not the texture is normal to the coloring and other principal features of the hand as a whole.

We have already stressed the importance of being on the lookout for marked differences in texture. We have done so not so much for its extreme importance in the final result, but rather to teach you to be observant. You must train yourself to overlook nothing that can be helpful to you in drawing a perfect mental picture of the hands you study.

Consistency of the Hands

The next important thing to consider in judging the whole hand is the consistency or "feel." Is the hand cold, or warm? Moist or dry? Hard or soft? Firm or flabby? Strong or weak? These points can be quickly determined by touching the lower part of the palm with the fingers and drawing these down toward the top. After that, grasp the hand as if in a hand clasp. In this manner you will get the response from the returned grip.

A hand to be normal should have a firmness of feel and a certain amount of moisture. The heat of the hand should be in ratio to the normal temperature of the body. You will soon be able to judge the difference between a hand too cold, too hot, too dry, too moist, just as you will be able to evaluate the firmness and softness.

First note the characteristics which go with a normal hand. Its firmness denotes strength of character and friendliness. Its warmth shows good health brought on through good circulation of the blood. With these important facts fixed in your mind, prepare to go forward, backward and sideways.

If the hand is unusually flexible, it denotes much adaptability, but hardly enough stability of purpose to make for complete reliability. If the hand is hard, stiff and unyielding, you find obstinacy.

People with flexible hands usually "bend before they break." In other words they do not fight impossible situations. However, because of that trait, they are liable to "quit" at the wrong time. Those with rigid hands "break before they bend." They sometimes "fight wind-mills," as did Cervantes' famous Don Quixote. By this we mean they put too much stress upon nonessentials, argue every point, no matter how small, and as a result, often lose sight of important issues.

If the hand is quite thick and fleshy, coupled with a hard, unyielding consistency, then there is the danger of selfishness and a desire to dominate.

If the hand is soft, flabby and unresponsive to a hand clasp, like a "dead fish," there is definite evidence of coldness and unreliability, snobbishness, lack of interest in others, egotism and often downright trickiness.

If the hand shake is overexaggerated then you are liable to be contacting a braggart and "blow-hard," one who has an over-exalted opinion of his own worth.

If the hand appears to be more fleshy than it should be in contrast with the rest of the body, you have love of pleasure and physical comfort.

A "skinny" hand is generally indicative of a nervous and sometimes an erratic nature.

A cold hand is to be associated with a person of rather poor circulation and lack of vitality, unresponsive in his emotions and enthusiasm. A very warm, slightly moist hand is just the opposite.

A hot, dry hand is nearly always associated with passion and a quick temper, which cools very quickly.

A warm, clammy hand is not a bad indication as many persons suppose. Rather the individual with such a hand is really friendly, but a bit backward in his friendliness. He has to be drawn out of himself by touching some responsive chord in his make-up. Once this is done you will find him very likeable.

The cold, clammy hand shows many of the tendencies of the warm, clammy hand, although a bit more exaggeratedly. Sometimes, though, this type of hand is made so by some physical deficiency that may affect the disposition.

Study these main points carefully and place them firmly in your mind before you proceed further. And, as always, remember to balance one truth against another.

Color of the Hand

The normal color of the hand should be "flesh." It should neither be too pinkish, nor too pale. A hand with normal coloring denotes general good health.

A hand more "pinkish or reddish" than normal is usually indicative of a full-blooded person. Such are generally warm hearted, impulsive, quick tempered and sometimes passionate people. Unusually red hands may indicate a violent temper with gross and strong materialistic tendencies. Persons with these hands are often subject to, or suffering from, disturbance in the circulatory system.

Remember this: The better the color of the hands—unless carried to extremes—the more optimistic, the more active and the better natured the subject.

Variations of the reddish color have definite meanings. A person with hands appearing "purplish," is often suffering from uncertain health with resultant sluggishness and inertia, both mentally and physically.

Hands which appear to have a "reddish-brown" coloring generally belong to those who have much ambition coupled with a keen mind. If this color is apparent in a lean, flat hand, it will invariably denote a domineering, overbearing nature.

The reverse indications, of course, are to be found in hands lacking in pigmentation—in light colored hands but rarely in those of a "yellowish" cast. The yellowish type of coloring belongs to the person who is high strung, impressionable and quite artistic. However, the yellow hand does not denote the vigor and ambition belonging to the brown or "reddish" hand. Those with yellow coloring are usually easily discouraged.

The less "reddish or pinkish" the coloring, the more are the indications of temperament opposite from the normal colored hands. For example: A very white hand denotes traits opposite from the hand of good color. Instead of activity you will find indolence. Pessimism instead of optimism. Nervousness instead of normal impatience, etc.

If the hand is "milk white" and apparently neither affected by heat or cold, or pressure, the owner, unless suffering from some serious anaemic condition, is usually quite cold and undemonstrative. With this type of hand you will also find egotism in varying degrees, exacting in demands to the point of petty tyranny and narrow-mindedness.

White, or extremely light colored hands, with many red or purple blotches, are indicative of a health difficulty, usually emanating from the circulatory or eliminative system.

There is one important fact to remember in judging the color of hands: The natural coloring of the person. You will naturally find reddish hands belonging to a person of florid complexion . . . pale hands with one usually fair, and yellowish hands coupled with a sallow face. However, these conditions, if normal, should not change your analysis. The persons possessing the colorings just mentioned, and others, will show the same tendencies in their general makeup as they do in their hands.

However, it is more important to note when there is a difference in coloring of the hands as compared with the face. Here is where you will obtain your first definite information in determining the primary classification of your subject.

Before we come to the study of the next division of Hand Analysis, go back over the preceding pages and review what you have read. In all the facts we have given so far, there are important fundamental truths . . . truths which must be learned and applied before anything further can be done toward a more complete study of the hands.

2

THE THUMB

The entire hand, the structure, texture and the many hieroglyphics which make up the lines in the palms of the hand, are "character revealers." This is especially true of the Thumbs.

"Thumbs Up!"

This expression, supposed to indicate courage, was made popular during World War II in countries whose people proved that they could take it.

In the early Christian era, when the followers of Christianity were literally thrown to the lions, the ruler of that day, sitting safely in his box in the arena, would indicate with the motion of his thumbs what the fate of the individual would be.

Thumbs down, meant that the victim's fate was sealed, and as the crowds, taking their cue from the Emperor, would cheer, the lions were loosed to carry out the Emperor's edict.

Thumbs up, meant the accused was spared, and again the crowd would follow the leader and cheer.

So, down through the ages, thumbs up or thumbs down, were not chance expressions.

The thumb on a person's hand truly reveals more of his character than any other part of his anatomy. It literally "sticks out like a sore thumb" telling those familiar with its characteristics, the story of strength or weakness.

"Thumbs Up!" A thumb that seems to be protruding even

when the hand is closed (Fig. 2-1) indicates courage and a fighting spirit, and goes further with this warning: "Look out. Don't push me too far, or I'll fight!"

Isn't that what England's people, who popularized this slogan during World War II, said in so many ways?

A high-set thumb, one that is set up on the hand (Fig. 2-2), is usually rigid. Contrary to general opinion, rigid thumbs do not always indicate stubbornness. If the entire hand is rigid, then a decided backwardness and self consciousness is revealed. But if the fingers and palm are flexible and the thumb is rigid, the expression "stubborn as a mule" will most likely fit. How's your flexibility?

A low set thumb, one that is set low on the hand, (Fig. 2-3) indicates a friendly, sociable person. Such an individual is usually an outgoing individual, a good mixer and should be doing work which brings him into contact with the public.

Take a careful look at TV personalities such as Ed Sullivan, Jack Paar, Bob Hope, Jack Benny, Arthur Godfrey, to name just a few who have remained on top for a long time. Watch their hands when they shake hands. They all have low set thumbs. Public relation executives also have this type of thumb. These people seem to exude friendliness and sociability.

Short thumbs, with blunt tips (Fig. 2-4), portray a "fussy" person. People with long thumbs are never quite satisfied. They are exacting bosses and insist on perfection in every job. Often they do not have the patience to do routine work. They have an insatiable curiosity and want to know the why's and wherefore's of everything.

Narrow-waisted thumbs, where the lower phalange is narrow, causing the joints to stand out (Fig. 2-5), belong to those who are inherently refined. They abhor coarseness or crudeness of any kind and like work where they are required to assume responsibility.

If your thumbs are flexible, you like friendly arguments. If the thumbs are rigid, you'll argue, but not in any friendly fashion.

A very large lower joint, where the thumb is joined to the hand (Fig. 2-6), marks the individual as a good politician, not

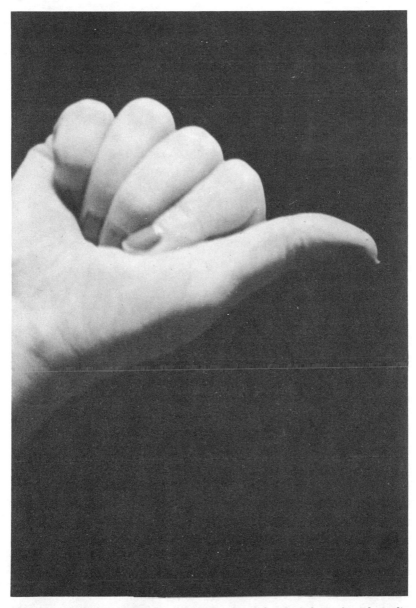

Fig. 2-1. Thumb protruding, even when the hand is closed, indicates courage and a fighting spirit.

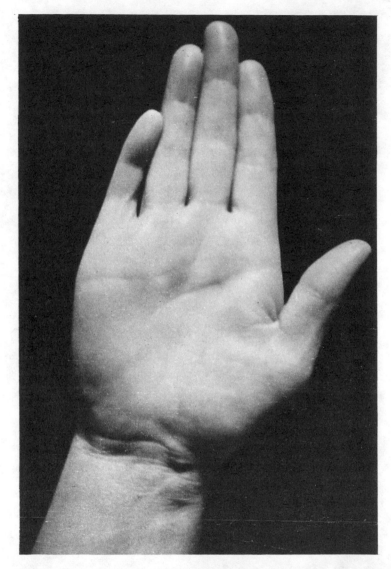

Fig. 2-2. A high-set thumb is usually rigid; but if the fingers and palms are flexible, stubbornness is indicated. If the entire hand is rigid, there is a decided backwardness and self-consciousness. The home-maker type woman has a high-set thumb that is quite rigid. She usually has a mind of her own and wants to be her own boss.

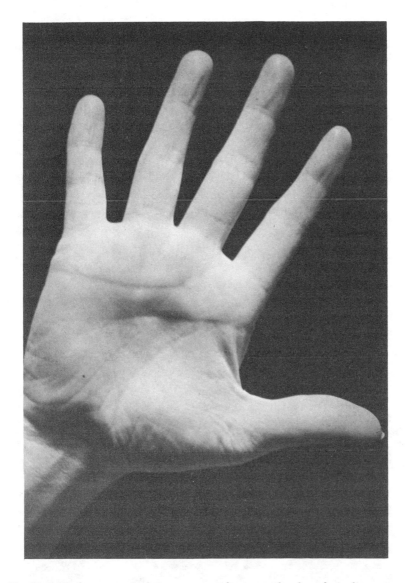

Fig. 2-3. A low-set thumb, one set low on the hand, indicates a friendly, social person, a good mixer. Many TV personalities and other public-contact individuals have this type of thumb. They exude friendliness.

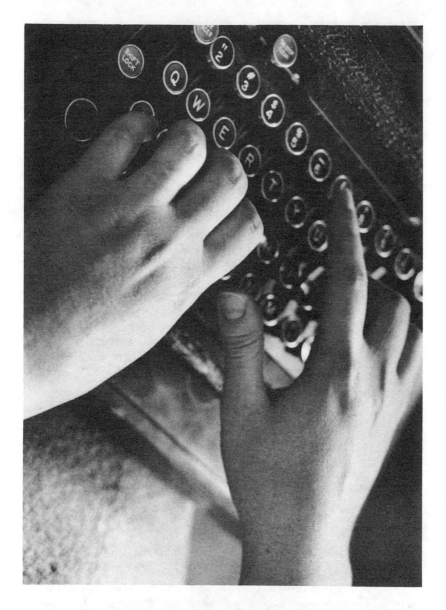

Fig. 2-4. Short thumbs with blunt tips belong to men and women capable of doing routine and precision work.

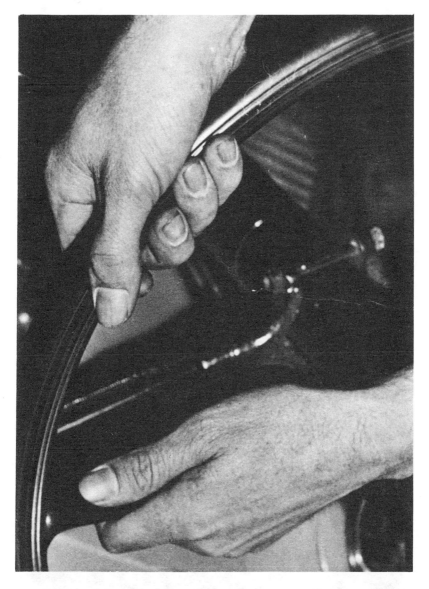

Fig. 2-5. Narrow-waisted thumbs, where the lower phalange is narrow, belong to those who are inherently refined and like work where they assume responsibility.

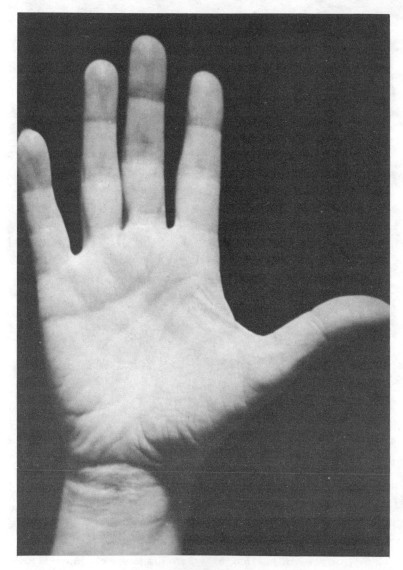

Fig. 2-6.

necessarily in politics. Such an individual usually has the uncanny ability to persuade others to his way of thinking.

A survey of women's hands have proved that the true homemaker type has a high set thumb, quite rigid (Fig. 2-2). She usually has a mind of her own and is pretty much her own boss.

Her career sister, who has to please her boss and others in her work, will have a low set thumb that is flexible (Fig. 2-6).

If the career woman is in business for herself, it's a safe bet her thumb will be low set and quite rigid.

When you are in crowds or are walking down the street, watch the way people carry their thumbs.

The man hurrying along with a briefcase under his arm will almost invariably keep his free hand half closed with the thumb sticking out. If he's a salesman, going out to tackle a tough customer, the hand will be clenched, but the thumb will still be prominent.

The pert little lady, who walks with quick, jerky steps, is likely to have the tip of her thumb clenched tightly to her hand (Fig. 2-7). Perhaps she has an appointment with her dentist, or some other disagreeable mission to perform, and she is clenching her thumb to keep her nerves from getting the better of her. My dentist tells me that most of his patients clench their thumbs while he works on their teeth.

Take a look at window shoppers, the ones just dawdling along, killing time (Fig. 2-8). It is their habit to carry the thumb loosely inside of the hand, which indicates mental relaxation.

The extreme of this attitude is when the entire hand is too relaxed. This usually represents the nerveless fingers and hands of an individual who has a serious nervous and mental deficency. If you look closely, you may see this subject's lips moving, as he frequently talks to himself.

If your dinner partner happens to have a high set, rigid thumb, you'd better get set to listen to the latest exploits of junior. If, perhaps, you want her to have a high opinion of you, try to talk intelligently about the price of home commodities and the high cost of food, for this type of an individual leans strongly toward home-making.

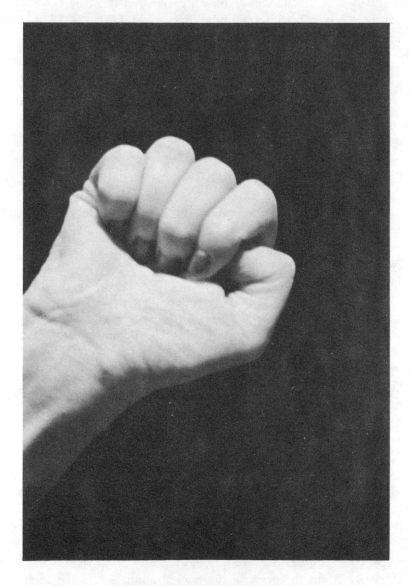

Fig. 2-7. Clenching the thumb shows tension and inner nervousness. This is often referred to as "holding our thumbs."

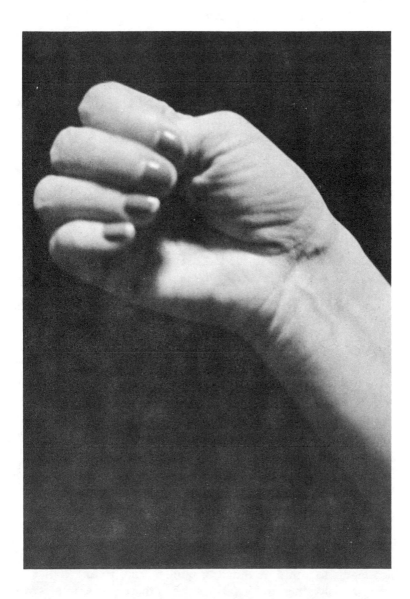

Fig. 2-8. "Carrying the thumb" in the palm indicates mental relaxation. The extreme of this represents a serious nervous and mental deficiency.

If the man behind the desk is a big, bluff man with a good sized hand and an extra large lower thumb joint, you will make friends and hold his attention by having a knowledge of public affairs, especially politics. But don't argue with him about his views. Passive resistance is your best weapon.

If the wife, your own or the boss's, has a pointed thumb, set high and rigid, don't try to pick out gifts for her. Just give her the money, with a sweet note, intimating that her taste and judgment is so much better than yours. The chances are she would find fault with anything you might choose.

If friend husband has a long, narrow-waisted thumb, don't expect him to be a handyman around the house. Above all, don't ask him to drive nails, or he is likely to bless you out when he hits his thumb.

If the boy friend has a short, thickset thumb which is rigid, and he loses his temper at the slightest provocation, don't expect him to grow wings after marriage. He was born with a temper as short as his thumb.

If the girl friend has a flexible, low set thumb, you can expect continued interest in her career. Housekeeping and domesticity will always come second in her consideration.

A little study will bring the realization that the Thumb does stand out, declaring a great deal about you and your character. The study of Thumbs, as outlined in the following pages, should prove very fascinating to you.

In the study of character by the aid of facial attributes, the eyes and nose play an important part. In Hand Analysis, the hand, in its entirety is considered in the same relation as the eyes, while the thumb is placed upon the same calculating basis as is the nose.

One of the primary essentials in reference to the thumb is this fact: The thicker, wider and larger the first joint, the more gross and materialistic is the individual. In reverse to this is the thumb which tapers to a thin, rounded or pointed end. Here is indicated more spiritual values and ideals. Between these two extremes you will find modifications.

A "good thumb" (Fig. 2-6) is one large enough to be in

proportion to the hand proper. It should be fairly slender and set medium high. The first joint should be a trifle longer then the second and not too thick or heavy at the end. The thumb should bend back, both at the first and second joints, but not too far. The middle of the second joint should be slightly narrow, giving it a "waisted" appearance. That type of thumb on a fairly good hand will be of the same relative assistance as a strong nose to a well shaped face.

The type of thumb, just described, typifies the following: well proportioned . . . intellectuality. Set fairly high . . . good ideals and inherent honesty. First joint longer than the second . . . will power but not stubbornness. Neither too thick, nor too thin at first joint . . . even balance between the spiritual and material. "Waisted" appearance in second joint . . . logic, reasoning power and diplomacy.

If the second joint is much longer than the first and decidedly "waisted" that thumb belongs to a person who is so logical that he can produce some of the most startling reasons why he should not do this or that. If the first joint is much longer than the second, then you have a person who is downright set in his ways, and logic or reason play but little part in this.

The Square Hand shows an outstanding example of a thumb that is seen more often than any other. It is found on a square, practical hand with long fingers, and very few lines on the palm. The lines are exceptionally deep, especially the heart line which goes all the way across the palm.

This man is an optimist. He has good coordination of mind and muscle. The joining of the Life Line and Head Line indicates that he will rule himself by reason and will also be cautious in driving.

The short first finger shows impatience, which however is kept in check by the straight Head Line.

It is interesting to know that this man has driven many thousands of miles with only one minor accident, and this was not the result of his own driving ability.

Take a good look at the nails, you will want to remember them when you make a study of the nails.

Here is another important fact. The distance the thumb stays away from the hand is often indicative of the mental alertness and brain activity.

It is a well known medical fact that infants always keep their thumbs tightly closed within their fingers until the mentality of the child begins to develop. Then the thumb begins to unfold.

Feeble minded persons also keep their thumbs tucked inside the palm (Fig. 2-7).

One of the first signs of an attack of epilepsy, in those subject to it, is the fingers starting to clasp over the inturned thumb.

The manner in which the thumb is held also reveals another trait . . . generosity or close-fistedness. Show us a person who holds his thumb close to the hand, but not necessarily inside of it and we will show you one who lacks generosity in one form or another (Fig. 2-8).

Take a close set thumb and add to it fingers tight together, turning upward at the ends so they form a cup-like appearance for the entire hand, and "Scotch" tendencies will usually prevail to the nth degree.

Now let us analyze the thumb. If the first joint is long and fairly large, then the governing force is the will. The person with this distinguishing mark is not easily influenced by emotions. If the size of the first joint is over-emphasized, then you have one who may be too determined and headstrong for his own best interests. If the first joint is long and tapers off at the end into a sort of blunt point, you will find considerable intuition and ability to follow a "hunch."

If the first joint is markedly shorter than the second joint, that person may be very obstinate and hard to convince. If this joint is broad and square to an unusual degree, it usually indicates a most unpleasant temper. If the first joint takes on a "club-like" appearance then most unpleasant traits are present, including ungovernable temper, brutality, grossness, animal cunning and obstinacy of the worst type. Fortunately you will seldom see the "club-like" thumb, particularly among intelligent people.

This repulsive looking digit is mostly synonymous to the "Savage or Primitive Hand." However, if it is seen, no matter how fine the other characteristics indicated may be, there is, lurking in the background somewhere, the tendencies it represents. Possibly, through self-discipline, these will never make themselves evident, but the threat of an outbreak from them still remains.

There is one important exception to this rule that must be given consideration. If the "club-like thumb" is found on a hand where every other characteristic belies its indications, then you will find it to be a peculiar family trait, handed down from generation to generation. And this aspect should certainly be given consideration before cataloging the subject.

Next to the "club thumb" is another, just as unpleasant in its significance. This thumb is extraordinarily broad and very square at the first joint. The person having such a thumb is capable of deep hatreds and a desire for revenge. It is not to be confused with the furious tempered "club thumb." The long, broad, thick thumb is that of the cold, calculating grudge carrier; one who never forgets a wrong and will avenge it in some way if it takes a lifetime.

A large thumb indicates independence in thought and in action. It belongs to the type who want to be "leaders" in one way or another. A small thumb is that of a sentimentalist, one apt to feel sorry for himself and often a "leaner," allowing someone else to assume responsibility. People with small thumbs often do a lot of talking about "their place in the sun," but seldom make any effort to achieve it.

A supple thumb, bending back easily at the second joint, is that of adaptability, friendliness, generosity and easygoing. If the first joint also turns backward to a marked degree, you have profligacy in many things; money, thoughts, friendships . . . in fact the possessor of such a thumb has a hard time saying "no." He can always be reached through his sympathy. He is generally too good a fellow for his own good. The type further indicates quick emotions, impulses and temper, but this is not a lasting type.

Possessors of firm jointed thumbs are usually cautious, practical and often hard to understand.

Large thumbs on women's hands couple clear thinking and practicability. The emotions, affections and loves are deep but are seldom displayed promiscuously. A large thumbed woman is nearly always sensible in all affairs of a business or administrative nature. She has an excellent sense of the value of money and knows how to spend it wisely.

The small thumbed woman is the more intriguing. Love, affection, passion are an integral part of her life. She shows her feelings in a pronounced way to every one for whom she may care.

Study thumbs carefully. Understand their meaning in ratio to the balance of the hand. After you have had a fair amount of experience with different types you will find you will be able to classify them almost at a glance. By having a firm understanding of the significance of thumbs you will possess a valuable asset in your further probing into the eccentricities of the hand.

3

THE FINGERS

Next to the thumb, the fingers are the most important item in the analysis of the whole hand. These must be studied very carefully before you can attempt to do anything with the palm.

After you are able to catalog the thumb, then you may study the length, size and shape of the fingers.

This is best done by letting the hand lie in a perfectly relaxed position. In this way you can get a good idea how the fingers drop into position when the hand is held normally.

Note whether the fingers have a tendency to lie fairly straight out, with little tendency to curve backward toward the palm in the first and second joints. Also see if the fingers "fan-out" to allow considerable space between each digit. Also notice if the thumb stands away from the hand.

A hand with these general characteristics is called a "relaxed hand." A person possessing such is "open-handed."

He will be quite generous in all things, rather easygoing in money matters, frank and fair in his dealings with others, optimistic and cheerful, warm hearted and friendly to all, and quite a "good fellow." If the fingers extend when the hand is relaxed, appearing almost straight, you will find a person of the "plunger" type . . . usually willing to take a chance on anything which looks good. This trait will be enhanced in ratio to the "spread" of the fingers. If, in the relaxed hand, the thumb closely hugs the palm, you will find traits of "good spending," but not extravagance. The "guarding" thumb is indicative of a desire to "save something for a rainy day."

If the fingers turn inward toward the palm and then set close together, you have tendencies directly opposite to the open hand. We have seen some exaggerated cases of the "closed hand," where it was held so closely together that the fingers actually overlapped, with the thumb setting firmly against the palm. That hand was always in a position as if it were ready to be used as a "cup" to pick up water. In every instance, we found that the person with this sort of hand, was downright stingy; not only with money, but with everything else worthwhile in life. One of the greatest faults found in people possessing the "cup-like" hand, is narrowness in outlook. They seldom, if ever, have vision. They cannot possibly see the other fellow's viewpoint because they will not make an effort to do so.

Each finger has been given a name; by whom, why and when, no one knows. About the most logical explanation we can give for the names of the fingers is this: In the distant past, when palmistry was considered more or less a "black art" everything about it had to be mysterious, so the fingers became known by the names of certain Planets and the Ancient Gods. The first, or index finger, was named Jupiter. The second, or middle finger, Saturn. The third, or ring finger, was called Sun, or sometimes Apollo, and the fourth, or little finger, Mercury.

True, the meaning of the names of the fingers do partake of some of the influences of the planets used in Astrological calculations, but hardly enough to warrant continued designation.

You can use your own judgment as to whether you prefer to call the fingers by their mythological names, or merely refer to them in the language we all understand . . . First, Second, Third and Fourth. We have always used the latter system and found it to be entirely satisfactory. Of course it might be well for you to learn the technical names, as you very probably will run across persons who have a smattering of palmistry and like to air their knowledge. If, with these people, you should show ignorance of the regulation names of the fingers, you might be considered ignorant.

Jupiter—*First or Index Finger:*   Here is found determination, patience, ambition, pride and spirit. It is the finger of the ego. *If it is long* it represents self-confidence, executive but diplomatic ability and pride of achievement. *If it is short* there is lack of patience. Too outspoken. Dislike of detail. A better order giver than order taker; *if it is excessive in length* it indicates conceit and overconfidence with dictatorial tendencies. It also indicates love of praise and unusual interests; *if it is crooked* the person will have very original ideas, but will have difficulty in carrying these plans to a successful conclusion.

Saturn—*Second or Middle Finger:* This is the finger of objectivity as related to material things in life . . . finance, success in business, professions, etc. *If it is long* there is a good assurance of success in things one has to work hard to achieve. The length of the finger also represents caution and prudence, together with careful planning; *if it is too long* cautiousness becomes procrastination and causes loss of many opportunities by not taking advantage of them. If this finger is extremely long, the individual may be subject to melancholy and have a rather morbid turn of mind; *if it is short* then there is but little promise of success in life. Financial difficulties and constant struggle for existence are the ultimate result; *if it is crooked and long* there is a tendency to frustrate one's own plans by poor judgment; *if it is crooked and short* there is inability to plan correctly.

Sun—*Third or Ring Finger:* This is the finger of art, beauty, music and love of the public. It is also a good indicator of friendliness, sympathy and emotions. *If it is long* the individual will have a decided artistic sense and inclination, although not necessarily an actual follower or participant in the arts. It also represents emotionalism in ratio to its length; *if it is too long* there will be love of notoriety, gambling and speculation. Passionate craving for affection. Emotionalism to a high degree with the "heart often ruling the head"; *if it is short* this shows that the individual is not overly friendly and has no particular desire for distinction. He has very little appreciation of the better things of life and usually is associated with a person who lacks appreciation of artistic things; *if it is crooked* it shows a retiring nature and one aloof to friendliness. This individual has little desire to mingle with people.

Mercury—*Fourth or Little Finger:* This is the finger that shows intellect and material things. It is usually in direct contrast to the meaning of the third finger. *If it is long* there will be good mental power and executive capabilities. Also ability of expression, either through the written or spoken word. This long, little finger is usually the mark of a militarist, politician, lawyer, writer and others who must possess the ability of clear expression of their ideas; *if it is too long* this indicates cleverness of ideas which can be sly. It is, however, not necessarily a dishonest indication; *if it is short* this shows quick perception and rapid thinking, but lack of stability and concentration; *if it is crooked* there will be a tendency to follow intuition and first impressions rather blindly. If very crooked then there is the tendency to jump at conclusions which are often erroneous.

As you study various hands, you will find that the fingers do not follow a straight line as they meet the palm. There is definite significance to this irregularity.

If the fingers are set on a slightly curved arc across the upper part of the palm so that the second and third fingers are in line, and with the first and fourth fingers dropping to such a point that they are also in line, you have the best possible arrangement. Fingers set like this indicate a rather even temper, good humor and freedom from undue worry. A person who has fingers set in this manner will go through life taking things as they come. He will meet life's problems sanely, and as a result will have pretty clear sailing. At least he will do very little to tear his life apart by needless stewing and fretting about things over which he has no control.

A finger set very low, as though it has been driven into the palm proper, is considered to have lost much of its power. For example, a very low set first finger is indicative of timidity, backwardness and extreme sensitiveness. The possessor of such a misplaced finger usually suffers dreadfully from the feeling that everyone is against him.

The second finger is seldom found to be out of place, nor is the third. However, if the second finger is low, it will indicate extreme moodiness almost bordering upon hysteria. If the third, or ring finger, is out of place you will find that it is a indication of lack of sympathy and understanding of another's troubles or sorrows.

When the fourth or little finger is set low, we have found the person to be quick tempered, but with an anger that cools as quickly as it comes. Some authorities on palmistry claim that a low set little finger indicates failure in life's struggles. We cannot agree with this latter interpretation as we have found low set little fingers in the hands of many very successful people.

It is better to have the finger fairly long in proportion to the length of the palm. This type of finger indicates a proper balance between careful planning and good execution. The hand of a successful businessman, or executive, is generally one with fingers slightly longer than the palm, and with a long index finger and little finger. The moderate length of all fingers gives the power to be particular in small things, and yet not be "fussy." The long index finger indicates executive ability and the long little finger the ability to handle people.

A large palm and short fingers, with bulging joints, is the hand of the skeptic. Short fingers, with fairly large hands, indicate neglect of detail; they can plan something in a big way, but do not have the patience to carry it out. This type of hand is often found in the successful attorney who can map out his case in general, but wants someone else to make up his briefs. After all the minute details are taken care of, he will go into court and handle the whole affair in a superb manner.

Long fingers are always indicative of love of detail. These are the fingers that delight in having everything just so. They belong to the person who believes that "anything worth doing is worth doing well." If the fingers are excessively long, that person is inclined to worry too much over trifles. If the palm is small and rather short in comparison to the fingers and also soft, then you have one who will always make mountains out of molehills.

At the inside ends of the fingers, as a general rule, you will find little cushions of flesh. These are indicators of sensitiveness and diplomacy. If these are overdeveloped, standing up like little pointed hills, you will find extreme sensitiveness. These individuals usually have to be handled with kid gloves for fear of offending them. Complete lack of these cushions, indicates a lack of diplomacy and also persons who are rather impervious to slights. These mounts, in the proper proportions are nearly always to be found in the hands of persons with an artistic temperament. They are also found in the hands of businessmen who govern their employees and customers with friendliness and tact, rather than by sheer power of will.

Fingers with first joints longer than the other two, are those of individuals who possess a great deal of natural intuition. If the fingers are long and flexible in these joints, you will find one who will do better to follow "hunches" or first impressions, rather than try to reason things out carefully.

If the fingers have a tendency to slope off rather abruptly at the tip, you have artistic sensibilities and talents in great abundance. This type of finger tip is very often found in a person with a natural ear for music or talent for dancing.

The stiffness of the fingers as related to the palm, tells of adaptability. Fingers that can be bent backward from the palm, are those of one who is easily adaptable to all conditions. These people bend in order to allow the storms and eddies of life pass over, or by them.

The individual with very stiff fingers is not adaptable. He will break before he bends. If the stiff fingered person goes down through any blow the fates may send, he usually stays down, or, at least, has a hard time regaining his feet.

The supple-fingered person bounds back from every buffet of life with the resiliency of a rubber ball.

4

THE MAP OF THE HAND

Figure 4-1 is a diagram of the inside of the right hand. You will notice that this covers the whole hand, including palm, fingers and thumb, and a short portion of the wrist, directly below the base of the palm. This diagram we will call the "map." It is very important for you to become familiar with this map so that you can always have a mental picture of it when you are looking at a hand.

You will notice we have divided each portion of the hand into sections with the meaning of each of these. Study this map thoroughly and carefully before you attempt to do the same for the other diagram on page 66 entitled the "lines."

In the map we have given you the usual names for each finger and each mount and also stated what each represents. As we said before, you can learn to call the fingers and other sections of the hand by the titles which are usually given to them by palmists, or you can merely designate these according to their real significance.

One of the best ways to familiarize yourself with the "map" is to remember this; the palm proper is divided into three distinct zones. Zone one lies in the section which includes the heart line as well as the area above it, and is known as the "Emotional Zone." The second zone lies directly below the Heart Line and covers that space down to and including the Head Line and is

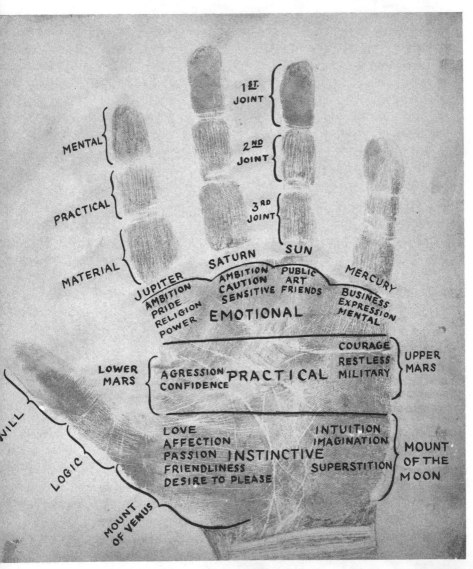

Fig. 4-1.

known as the "Practical Zone." Zone three, is the whole portion of the hand below the Head Line to the wrist and is known as the "Instinctive Zone."

The proof of the accuracy of these divisions can be proven as follows: A hand that may appear to have a high development in the "Emotional Zone" (through prominence of the flesh directly below or near the base of the fingers) will nearly always belong to a person who is highly emotional in one way or another. This emotionalism may express itself in sympathy, impulsiveness in doing good, strong expressions of joy or sorrow, or even in a quick temper of short duration. This emotionalism will be unusually developed if there appears to be little prominence in the protuberances in the rest of the hand.

If the middle part of the hand, or the "Practical Zone" gives indication of being developed then you are in contact with one who is not ruled by emotions, but by common sense and matter-of-fact reasoning. If the lower part of the hand is highly developed so that the lower inside of the palm and the cushioned part around the base of the thumb seem to stand out very prominently, then "instinct" is playing a great part with that individual. Such persons are naturally, or "instinctively" friendly and have a sincere desire to please all with whom they come in contact. They are usually quite intuitive and sometimes have an almost uncanny ability of sensing the right or wrong thing. If there is unusual development on the cushioned part of the palm, near the base toward the inside, you may find some instinctive superstitions and rather peculiar beliefs.

The best way to determine the predominance of the zones of the hand, is to extend the hand to its fullest. In this manner, by sighting along the palm, from the fingers toward the wrist, you can readily ascertain the relative height or flatness of the various sections of the palm.

Sometimes the hollow of the palm appears to be off balance or leaning in one direction or another. We have found, in our experience, that this leaning has a rather definite meaning. If the hollow is leaning toward the Life Line, there are oftentimes troubles with the family which have caused a person to leave home rather early in life. If the hollow is leaning toward the Fate Line, then there are struggles against unkind and unpleasant conditions over which one has no control. If leaning toward the Head Line, there is nervousness and always the possibility of nervous disorders. Leaning toward the Heart Line, shows difficulties throughout life with friends and others in whom one puts confidence and trust.

In the diagram marked "The map of lines" on page 66, we have shown you the seven principal lines. There are seven others of lesser importance which will be discussed later. First, it is important to familiarize yourself with the main lines. At first glance, you may believe it will be rather difficult to understand the meaning of the lines because you will never find any sets of these exactly alike in any hand. However, you can obtain a fair idea as to how the principal lines should look in order to be normal, by careful study of the "map of lines." Deviations from this order, and you will encounter many, will have a very definite meaning that will be explained as we go along.

When you begin the study of the lines, you start the most fascinating part of palm analysis. You are seeing the threads of a great tapestry . . . the tapestry of a human life. It is these lines, their study and interpretation which makes palm analysis so extremely interesting. You will not learn to decipher the meaning of these lines in a day, a week, a month, or even a year. But, by constant study, the same as you have to do with anything else worthwhile, you will gradually arrive at a place where the lines do tell you a clear and accurate story . . . a story so interesting that you will be well repaid for all the effort you have gone to in order to read it.

5

THE PRINCIPAL LINES

We have chosen a hand print from our large collection to illustrate The Map of the Principal Lines (Fig. 5-1). We are doing this for two reasons: First—The lines shown are exactly as seen in a typical hand . . . not stiff, stilted and precise as these would be if a "line drawing" was used. Second—By studying this "Map" you may familiarize yourself with the general appearance of the lines as these are typical of the average hand. We selected this particular hand print because it shows clearly the Seven Principal Lines. It reveals the general contour and shape of the main lines and their relation one to the other.

This Map also gives the exact measurement of the thumb and fingers, showing the balance between each and their relativity to the palm . . . its length and breadth. This Hand is almost perfectly balanced, with the first and second fingers being practically of equal length and the thumb (measured from the outside, from the tip to the base of the second joint) is of equal length to the third finger.

The Seven Principal Lines shown in this Map, in order of importance are: No. 1—The Life Line. No. 2—The Head Line. No. 3—The Heart Line. No. 4—The Fate Line No. 5—The Bracelets. No. 6—The Marriage Line. No. 7—The Career Line. No. 8—Intuition.

Note: The Bracelets are drawn in on this Hand Print, as it

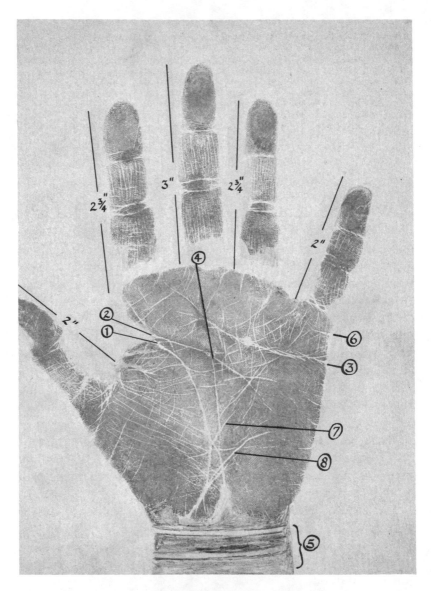

Fig. 5-1. Hand print showing principal lines.

is quite hard to get an impression of these in connection with the whole hand. However, these are clearly explained later on.

In analyzing the Lines proceed in the rotation just mentioned, starting with the Life Line and ending with the Career Line.

Lines to be perfect (and these are seldom seen) should be faintly pink in color, clearly defined, not too deeply cut and free from breaks or unusual disturbances. Very pale lines, almost imperceptible and sometimes whitish, usually denote poor circulation or some similar blood disturbance.

Very red lines are those of unusually full blooded people who may suffer from the heat and be subject to high blood pressure, even apoplexy. Yellowish lines indicate reserve and pride with sluggish elimination. Dark brown lines indicate a very emotional person who may not quickly forgive a wrong. Pink lines are the definite marks of cheerfulness and optimism. If lines of this color are in good condition (unbroken) life is generally quite pleasant. Broad, dark lines show quick temper with passions not easily controlled. Pale, broad lines generally represent uncertain health and individuals having these may be critically ill at any time.

Strange as it seems, lines often change in color, length, depth and even in course. Health conditions often bring about marked differences in the color of the lines and will sometimes shorten or lengthen them. This is particularly true of the Life, Heart and Head Line.

You must not take any single line as significant of the whole temperament, character, disposition or possibilties. All lines must be synthesized, each with relation to the other.

We may compare the hand to a fascinating "jig-saw puzzle." Each part has a direct meaning on the whole. However, each part by itself means little. All sections must be assembled before we see the picture or design of the component whole.

The right hand carries the most important information. However, you cannot neglect the left hand, as it definitely supports the right hand. Many persons consider the left hand as that of the past . . . the right hand representing the future. This is true, but to a limited extent.

We have found that the left hand will quite often reveal

incidents and happenings early in life from birth to the 15th year, and sometimes as far as the 20th year. In the left hand is often etched the story of life when the individual was under the supervision and jurisdiction of parents, relatives or others who more or less moulded the course of life in its formative stages. Illness and accidents in childhood, early life and adolescence will often be seen more clearly in the left hand than in the right.

Broadly speaking, the left hand is "The Original Plan." That is why marked discrepancies are often seen in the shape, length, contour and general conditions of the lines in the two hands. These differences are brought about by changes in temperament and disposition as one progresses from early life into maturity. For example, you may see a distinct talent indication in the left hand, and not find it in the right hand which clearly means that nothing was done to develop that talent. Or, impulsiveness and quick temper may show plainly in the left hand and be absent in the right. Here the significance is obvious . . . through discipline and self-control these traits have been mastered. Sometimes you may find many lines in the left hand and comparatively few in the right. This is generally a sign of extreme nervousness, restlessness or illness early in life which has been overcome. These markings may sometimes be reversed, with the right hand having the heavy lines and the left hand just a few. Then the meaning is opposite . . . calmness in earlier life and nervousness and restlessness later on, either through circumstances beyond their control or by worry and lack of mental poise.

Here are a few things we have found which are just about one hundred percent accurate in the left hand. A long, well defined Life Line, which runs deeply around under the base of the thumb represents long life and good health in the ancestry. If the lines fork at the bottom, with part of it going around under the base of the thumb and the other half running toward the lower center of the palm, stopping before it comes to the bottom, then there will be long life on one side of the family . . . moderate length of life on the other. A Life Line breaking in the left hand and then starting again, either in the same relative position, or a little to the right or left is almost infallible in this meaning. Either one or more very severe illnesses in early life, the death of a parent, or some other disturbance over which the individual had no control that greatly affected the latter life.

A line in the left hand, dropping down from either the Heart or Head Line, on a slant toward the inner base of the palm, shows the influence, or lack of influence of the father in early life. If the line is very long and appears to go to the wrist, or over the side of the hand, you will usually find the father was quite an influence in one way or another. If this line is short, the influence will not be strong. We have found this short line to mean that the father died or moved away when the individual was quite young. Disturbances such as lines cutting across, squares, an island etc., on the Life Line before it gets to a point between the 1st and 2nd fingers, will show childhood illnesses. A straight line coming up from the percussion side, or left side of the hand, low on the lower part of the palm, is often found on the hands of people who are foreign born. This is particularly accurate if the lines of water travel (explained later) are quite distinct.

Now returning to the lines proper and their significance, remember this . . . forks on the main lines, always give greater power. For example, a fork at the end of the Life Line indicates good health to the end of life and usually activity in the latter years of life. A fork of the Head Line gives greater mental power and also denotes mental versatility. A fork on the Heart Line is significant of a good heart and also shows a capacity for friendships and true affection.

If there are a myriad of lines in a hand, running in every direction, giving the appearance of a spider web, you have a person who worries and frets about everything. Very few lines show the calm person who is little affected by slight worries and trifles.

A hand that has very deeply carved lines, with rather a shriveled appearance, is almost a sure sign of a severe fever in early life.

The Life Line

As stated before, the first principal line to consider is the Life Line because it is by far the most important single line in the hand. Here is the start and finish of your actual being upon this conscious plane of existence. The Life Line tells the story of your health, your activities, your failures, your accomplishments; the past, the present and in some instances, the future.

The Life Line starts at the right side of the palm between the first finger and the thumb and swings across the palm around and down to the base of the palm. Looking at its general length and condition, you have a fair idea about the length and type of life the individual will have.

One of the first things to do in analyzing a Life Line is to divide it into parts representing periods of time. This is accomplished by first establishing an imaginary center in the middle of the Mount of Venus (the section of the hand enclosed in the Life Line) and then, from that point radiate other imaginary lines across the Mount of Venus toward the Life Line. (See print showing Principal Lines.) By this method you can break up the Life Line into periods of decades (10 year periods) and by so doing obtain a fairly accurate idea about the past, present or future.

Always remember this . . . it is extremely difficult, if not impossible, to accurately establish time in palm analysis. You can only estimate the approximate period, such as "in the vicinity of the twentieth year," or "between the thirty-third and the thirty-fifth year." Because of this difficulty of definitely calculating time, never "put yourself on a spot," by making a flat statement that such and such a thing happened at a specific time, or those who take particular delight in tripping anyone may discredit you.

It is always best to explain that you must estimate time. In that way you make yourself safer against the "show-me and the smart-alecky" type individual whom you will often meet if you go far into the practice of palm analysis.

From the indications of the Life Line, it is also not a good policy to make any definite statements pertaining to possible illnesses, disasters or early death as there is always a chance that you may be wrong in your deductions. Furthermore, it is our opinion that unpleasant things should not be stressed. True, there are many people who insist that they want to know everything, and will often ask you if you see "anything bad." But the majority of individuals do not want to hear about such things and even those who claim they do, actually do not. Foretelling morbid things by some palmists is one of the reasons why the science has been brought into disrepute. Therefore, it is wise to soft pedal much of the unpleasant aspects that the hand may reveal.

The average person believes that a short Life Line means a short life. This is not true, as we have often proven. We have seen many a Life Line which indicated, according to the length, only an age of thirty-five or forty in the hand of a person of fifty, sixty and older. In nearly every instance where this has occurred, we have discovered that the individual's life has been uneventful and rather drab.

A broken Life Line does not always mean sickness or death. Quite the contrary, it may represent some very radical change in a life; a complete change of location, business, occupation, marriage, divorce, etc. What this change may have been, or may be, is usually determined by markings and indications on other lines.

The closer the Life Line runs to the base of the thumb, the closer that individual's life stays to its original surroundings and the more restricted the activities.

By the same token, the farther across the hand the Life Line runs, the wider the activities, the broader the scope of life and farther a person goes from the original place of birth and environment. If the Life Line runs so far across the hand that it ends on the left of the center of the palm, there is a certain indication of success in life—above average. We have seen such a line often in the hands of both men and women who have gained either local, state or national reputation and honor.

Another fact that proves our contention on this point, is if you find a Life Line originally starting out as though it was going to stay very close to the base of the thumb, then suddenly breaking at some point and beginning again further into the center of the palm and continuing on, more to the middle, or across the palm, then you will find a person who had a change in the life which brought it more into the open than it had been before the break. This break is quite common in the hand of a woman, who after being widowed or divorced, came out of the wife and house-keeper class into real activity in the business world and has been successful in her undertakings. You can get a fair idea of the time of the change by using the system of decade division.

Now, for some of the most significant indications shown by the Life Line: When it rises far over on the outside of the hand and about halfway between the base of the index finger and the thumb, it represents close connections with the family. Even if seen in the hand of an older person, you will find that individual has always had a close association with the family, even though the immediate circle has been badly decimated by death. However, if the line starts high upward toward the base of the first finger, the meaning is reversed. Usually such a line shows sever-ance of contact with the family early in life and very little connection since that time.

If the Life Line and Head Line are closely connected at the beginning, you have a person who is cautious and prudent. The further the Head Line goes into the Life Line, the more pro-nounced are these traits.

When the Life and Head Lines are separated at the start of the Life Line, it shows self-confidence and independence, sometimes bordering on the impulsive. This marking is very essential for people who are in, or hope to gain positions of responsibility. If the Head Line is straight and also separated, that person is well fitted for public life or any executive or authoritative position.

You will occasionally find the Heart, Head and Life Lines all joined. If this conjunction takes place high on the hand, under the index finger, it generally signifies that a strong will, good mind and sympathy play a prominent part in this individual's life. On the surface he may appear brusque, but underneath he is kind, and even soft.

When the Life Line starts very close to the thumb and stays close to the Mount of Venus (thus diminishing the size) you have indications of either barrenness in a woman, or sterility in a man.

When a line connects the Life Line to the Fate Line, this is the mark of unusual protection against accident or bodily harm. Also, if the Life Line is strong, well marked and long, a person possesses rather remarkable recuperative powers and has much resistance to disease.

Sometimes, in a woman's hand, particularly if she is nearing middle age or passed it, you will find a branch on the Life Line. This is quite a good criterion as to how she will, or has passed through her "change period." The color of the line, in the region of the branch indicates the severity or lack of seriousness of the condition.

A Life Line ending very abruptly is indicative of a quick, not necessarily accidental, passing out of life. If the line is strong and long it will mean a long, healthy life with a very quick exit. When the line is distorted, or has many fine lines at the end, the indication is the opposite. Even though the meaning of certain marks is regarded to be quite accurate, these still may be wrong and it is rather senseless and a little cruel to tell anyone something unpleasant. It will do them no good, and always remember this . . . your interpretation may be faulty and *you may be wrong.*

Lines which rise or fall from the Life Line are indications of events in a life. If these lines point toward the fingers they are restrictions and disappointments, when they branch toward the wrist they indicate progress and activity.

A cross touching the Life Line means trouble with the family, death in the family or death of a close friend. If that cross lies between the Life Line and the thumb, it indicates a narrow escape for the individual, usually through a sudden illness or accident.

Tiny dots, either whitish or blue white in color, indicate uncertain health or exposure to danger. We have found those dots quite frequently in the hands of men who have been in war and under fire, or working in some hazardous undertaking. You can tell by the position of these dots on the line, just about the age when these incidents occurred.

When lines rise sharply from the Life Line and run in the direction of any mount, or unusual development, talent is to be found in accordance to the meaning of each mount. (See chapter of Mounts.) If the lines run all the way to the mount then the talent, or development has been put to good use.

A Life Line that has a wide branch toward the bottom means a life that branches out into wider activity and scope as the years go by.

If a line branches off the Life Line and runs downward, toward, or into the inside base of the palm (the Mount of the Moon) you will find a person who is restless and desirous of change, travel, etc. Such a line is often indicative of changes and travel.

In the foregoing we have given you the salient points of interpretation for the Life Line. However, there are many more things to be taken into consideration and the following is a short and concise review of what has already been said with other added important reckonings.

IF . . . The Life Line is well defined, deep and unbroken . . . then . . .
Fine Health, Strong Vitality and Good Character.

IF . . . The Life Line is broken in places . . . then . . .
Abrupt changes in the destiny of life.

IF . . . The Line appears to have many fine lines running away from it, both up and down . . . then . . .
A nervous temperament and possible uncertain health as a result.

IF . . . The Line is fairly straight and with little curve . . .
then . . .
The Emotions at all times are well under control.

IF . . . It is deeply curved around the base of the thumb . . . then . . .
One is highly emotional.

IF . . . The Life Line is extremely long, but thin . . . then . . .

An even, placid disposition, but not a great deal of vitality.

IF . . . It is extremely long and broad . . . then . . . Great vitality and excellent health.

IF . . . Very short and with very few other lines . . . then . . .

A life that goes along smoothly, but is rather uneventful.

IF . . . Accompanied by other parallel lines, so as to appear double . . . then . . .

An unusually healthy life and good indications for success.

IF . . . The Life Line runs into the wrist . . . then . . . Assurance of unusual length of life.

IF . . . It runs across the hand to the Mount of Luna . . . then . . .

Great activity in life and success . . . also much travel abroad.

IF . . . It starts above the Head Line . . . then . . . Great energy and dynamic personality.

IF . . . It branches upward, at the beginning, toward the index finger . . . then . . .

Perseverance and determination which will conquer all things.

IF . . . It has a cross at the beginning . . . then . . . An accident, or serious illness early in life.

IF . . . There is a square on the Life Line . . . then . . . A disappointment of some unusual nature.

IF . . . There is an "island" or other rough circular mark . . . then . . .

A run down system, or sometimes a nervous breakdown.

IF . . . It is cut across by very distinct and heavy lines . . . then . . .

Often a sign of a serious major operation.

IF . . . These lines run straight across . . . then . . .

Important changes, such as location, work, profession, etc.

IF . . . The Life Line gets stronger as it progresses . . . then . . .
Better health and increased confidence.

IF . . . The Line is very deep, broad and dark in color . . . then . . .
Strong, passionate nature, one ruled by impulse and instincts, rather than higher motives.

As we said at the beginning of this chapter, the Life Line is the most important single line in the hand. From it other conditions must be considered. However, the Life Line does not tell the whole story, as every other Line has its distinct meaning. But, everything else dovetails into the Life Line. Therefore, it is most important to "know your Life Line," and to know it as thoroughly as possible. After you can read the tale of the Life Line, you will find the interpretation of the other portions of the hand easier.

The Head Line

We look always to the Head Line to determine whether or not a person is fairly well adjusted to the conditions under which he lives. It tells us quite clearly the mental processes, the keenness or dullness of intellect, the capacity for clear thinking, nervousness, depression, etc. Next to the Life Line it is the most important line in the hand and therefore should be studied and analyzed after you have finished with the Life Line.

The Head Line, or Line of Thought, usually begins at three different places—under the index finger (Jupiter), near or at the Life Line, or inside the Life Line. Later on we will mention a few of the places where we have seen it start and explain what we have found to be the meaning, but for the present we will confine ourselves to the conventional rising of this Line.

To have the Head Line originate under the index finger is one of the best symbols. When it starts here and the Line is clear and straight, it gives good brain power, consecutive thinking, the ability of close concentration, practical determination and the power of self-rule. This type of line shows reason, logic and good judgment.

We mentioned in the previous pages the significance of a space between the Head and Life Line at their origin. If this space is unusually marked, an eighth to a quarter of an inch or more, then you have a rash, hasty disposition—an individual who acts before he thinks, someone who is very impatient and cannot wait for things to take their natural course. People with this sort of Head Line are the type who believe that "Rome was built in one day." This sort of Head Line on the hand of a woman often indicates a tendency to speak out of turn, and also to indulge in idle and sometimes malicious gossip. When the two lines are far apart you usually find a rather suspicious tendency and sometimes a gift of intuition. This latter trait will be highly developed if the Line of Intuition (see Map of Principal Lines) is plainly marked in the hand. With the Intuitive Line in the hand, the person with the "wide apart" Life and Head Lines has enough impulsiveness to warrant carrying out "first impressions."

Where the Head Line is long and dips down sharply toward the Mount of the Moon (the place of Inspiration, Instinct and Imagination) you generally have a person who is a dreamer. This type of Head Line is often found in the hand of a writer, poet, inventor and scientist. This type of Head Line, almost without fail, reveals creative ability of some sort. In studying this sort of Head Line you must be careful to differentiate between the DIP of it . . . if the Line runs all the way into the Mount of the Moon, not merely dipping toward it, you have an unfavorable indication. Such a person is dissatisfied with life in general, crying out "for a little spot of green and a patch of blue," but never making a sincere effort to acquire it. These people are usually the "defeatist" type, feeling life has been unkind; that fate has played tricks upon them. They have vague ideas, and sometimes highly imaginative notions as to what is wrong with the world, but are never practical enough to try to put their thoughts into action. They are the "sensitives and neurotics," with nervous disturbances which may lead to hysteria, insanity and self-destruction.

A Head Line that is very deep, unwavering and has little or no disturbance upon it, is the sort that makes for little or no mental disturbances. People with this sort of line are usually of a "one track mind." They have the ability to concentrate, but only on one thing at a time. If the line wavers, falters, twists and turns, then the reverse is conceded . . . scattered thoughts, lack of concentration, nervousness. A Head Line that forks at the end shows a versatile mentality, expanding and developing as the years go by. This is more true in the event the Line is straight and true in its earlier part.

Going back again to the type of Head Line that is separated from the Life Line . . . if you find such a condition, with the Head Line turning up sharply into the Mount of Jupiter, you have an independent person, one who cares little about public opinion, and will do as he pleases. You can't drive this type of person, but you can usually reach him through kindness and an appeal to his sympathy. If this combination of lines is found in a Spatulate Hand, or one with large knuckles and a great deal of daylight between all the phalanges of the fingers, you then have one who would be almost radical in his ideas and opinions. This is the mark of the reformer and iconoclast.

When the Head Line rises inside the Life Line that is over close to the thumb in such a way that it cuts across the Life Line as it comes over the palm, then you have fretfulness, worrying, nervousness and constant trouble over imaginary grievances. Fortunately this type of line is seldom seen.

Occasionally you may run across only a Head Line in a hand, with seemingly no Heart Line. In this case, the Head and Heart Lines are really one. This marking tells of either great success or failure. When a person with such a line determines upon a certain course he will usually carry it out in spite of all opposition or reasoning. If this is accompanied by a good Fate and Sun Line there is every indication of success, but if the Fate and Sun Lines are lacking or these are badly disturbed, failure will often come through errors of hasty action and faulty judgment. People with a combined Head and Heart Line are seldom understood by others and as a result sometimes find themselves quite alone in life.

A Double Head Line has unusual significance. We have seen this in the hands of people who have unusual mental capacity. The two lines run parallel and close to each other and yet do not touch. If they do touch, but only in one or two places, then this marking is conducive of a double mentality, where one is both determined and passive, sensitive and hard.

The principal points to remember about the Head Line are these: Straight, clear and unbroken indicating good practical sense and a love of things more material than theoretical. This type of line always represents a mind that works on a basis of "logical progression to reach a definite conclusion." All deviations from this type of a line are indicative of weaknesses of various sorts in contrast with this meaning. A Head Line that runs perfectly straight and all the way across the hand reflects an argumentative, determined mind . . . one who believes he is always right. Couple this with a low set and stubborn thumb, and you will have a very obstinate person . . . one who will listen to no other voice than his own.

When the Head Line appears to pursue two courses, that is the first half straight and the second sloping, or if there is a line which slopes off the Head Line in the general direction of the Mount of the Moon, then you find a practical nature in some respects, but highly imaginative in areas. This is the type of line so often seen in the hands of successful architects, builders and structural engineers. The straight part of the Head Line dominates the extreme practicability of the profession, while the slope gives them the necessary imagination and creative power to design what they build.

If there are branches on the Head Line drooping downward, you will find moodiness and pessimism. If the branches go upward toward the Heart Line, then you will find cheerfulness and optimism.

We mentioned at the beginning of this discussion on the Head Line, that you will often find this line starting in rather unusual places. Here are a few examples: Starting at the near middle of the hand and short . . . lack of clear thinking. Starting at a point high in the hand and quite near the Heart Line . . . jealousy and pettiness to an unpleasant degree. Starting low in the hand . . . about in line with the thumb joint, and running at an angle toward the little finger . . . great imagination. If the Intuitive Line is well marked in both hands, these individuals usually possess some unusual mental power, such as the commonly called "sixth sense."

Branching off the Heart Line in the region of the second or third finger, there will be an intensity of emotion which often affects the mind to such an extent as to make one dwell too much in the past. In all our years of experience we do not recall finding any other beginnings of the Head Line, except these, plus the conventional type:

A wavy Head Line denotes a changeable, erratic and rather unstable temperament.

Loops, circles, dots and islands on the Head Line denote headaches, neuralgia and poor memory.

If the Head Line is broken, or badly disturbed there has usually been some severe mental strain or nervous breakdown.

If the Head Line is darker in color than the other lines, and is distorted, or twisted . . . then there is a bad temper.

Now we give you some other significant facts concerning the Head Line:

IF . . . "Chained" at the beginning . . . then there is extreme nervousness and sensitiveness in early life.

IF . . . Decidedly curved . . . then . . . Impulsiveness and affection.

IF . . . Twisting and turning . . . then . . . Irresolution and indecision. Unable to make up the mind.

IF . . . Very pale and indistinct . . . then . . . Easily tired mentally . . . lack of vision.

IF . . . Intercepted by short line . . . then . . . Undeveloped mentality . . . lack of educational training.

IF . . . Intercepted by long, deep lines . . . then . . .
Shocks to the nervous system.

IF . . . It lies low in the hand . . . then . . .
Cheerfulness and much optimism.

IF . . . It lies high in the hand and near the Heart Line . . .
then . . .
The "head" usually rules the "heart."

IF . . . Connected to the Heart Line with one or more
lines . . . then . . .
An even balance between the Head and Heart.

In studying the Head Line, you must always consider the type of hand in which it lies. A strong Head Line in the strong square, spatulate or philosophic hand is increased twofold in its significance. This is true of a strong Head Line in the conic or nervous hand. A strong Head Line in a weak hand strengthens the whole hand, and so, in turn, a weak Head Line in a strong hand weakens it.

The Heart Line

The Heart Line always originates under the Fourth or Little Finger. Some palmists of the old school claim that it ends at this point, however, through the study of thousands of hands, we have found that such is not the case. As the Heart Line mainly governs the emotions, it is logical to believe that it should originate in the house of emotion (sometimes called Marriage) which occupies that space between the base of the little finger and the Heart Line.

The Heart Line usually ends at three points: Under the first finger (Jupiter); between the first and second fingers (Jupiter and Saturn), or under the second finger (Saturn). Occasionally, you will find the end under the third finger which is never a good place for the Heart Line to end. This represents selfishness of the worst sort; the type of person who would resort to all manner of hypocrisy to gain his ends.

Before going into the discussion of the ending of the Heart Line, let us consider the Line itself and its meaning toward the hand as a whole.

As stated before, the Heart Line has to deal primarily with the emotions, that is; affection, friendships, generosity, faithfulness, loyalty and those attributes which are usually associated with the Heart. It very often tells a tale concerning the organ proper.

The Heart Line, like all others, should be of good color and free from breaks and disturbances in order to have balance in emotions. A long Heart Line is always more desirable than a short one.

A long, strong Heart Line has as its basic indication—loyalty, trust and sincerity. A short Line just the reverse—shallowness, distrust and jealousy.

When the Heart Line sweeps across the hand with an upward fling at its end, either under or between the first or second fingers you will find optimism—the ability to come back from spells of depression very quickly and a good sense of humor. This is particularly true if the little finger is rather long and pointed. If the Heart Line swings downward at its end, toward the Head Line, then you find a more intense nature, one inclined to take life rather seriously and whose emotions are usually ruled by the Head.

The higher in the hand the Heart Line lies, the stronger the emotions. The lower and closer to the Head Line, the more reserved are these emotions.

If the Heart Line and the Head Line join at any place, then there is an undemonstrative nature, rather cold and distant, but one of strong, lasting affections and sincere friendships which seldom come to the surface except in periods of stress.

When the Heart Line swings across the hand from its rise, and ends under the first finger (Jupiter) you will find affections and love placed upon a definitely idealistic plane. Very little of so-called "passion" enters into the lives of those having this type of Heart Line. There is more desire for a union of "mind and spirit," than merely physical attraction. Men or women with this type of Heart Line place the object of their affection upon a pedestal and sometimes worship them from afar. If that ideal falls, if the "idol has clay feet," there is often a hurt which never heals.

When the Heart Line goes in a straight line entirely across the palm and ends a little above the Head Line and under the first finger, then you find both virtue and fault. The virtue is loyalty —the fault is "blind loyalty." This is the mark of individuals who cannot believe ill of the persons in whom they believe and they will fight to defend them to the last ditch. They will sacrifice in every way so that the ones they idolize may be well provided for, but when their eyes are once opened to the faults which they have either not seen, or refused to recognize, they are everlastingly through with those people. Nothing the offender can ever do will restore that person to their good graces.

When the Heart Line sweeps up between the first and second fingers, love, affection and friendships are not so idealistic, but very strong. Here is indicated a possessive sort of affection, the kind that will fight to hold on to the object of their devotion. You will find this type of Heart Line in the hands of men and women who will fight with the fury of savage beasts when some member of the opposite sex trespasses upon their property. There is always some jealousy connected with this type of line, but not the blind unreasoning sort to be found in the Heart Line that ends abruptly, or swings up quickly to the second finger.

The person with this type of Heart Line is primarily sensuous in emotions. These emotions do not come from the heart, but rather from pure physical attraction. As a result there is fickleness in the disposition—a constant desire to explore new pastures. Dangerous jealousy is predominant. Unless this type of Heart Line lies very close to the Head Line, you have a person who may "shoot and then think about it." If this Heart Line is close to the Head Line, you have a schemer—particularly in women. If this line is bare, deep and strong, then that woman will use all of her physical charms to catch and hold a man for material reasons only.

A Double Heart Line will always increase the strength of the indications of the general run of the Line.

Breaks in the Heart Line indicate disturbances in emotions, islands of fine lines will mean the same.

When the Heart Line is very red, out of proportion in color to the other lines, the meaning can be two-fold; either direct disturbance in the circulation with heart trouble, high blood pressure, or it can mean violence in both temper and affections. This last condition must be corelated to where the line ends. You will find less of the latter attribute predominating if the Heart Line ends under the first finger than you will find if it ends under the second finger.

If there is a cross or square on the Heart Line, you will usually find that death has taken a loved one. If these touch the Head Line then there has been, in the broad sense, tragedy in the life of the subject which may have been the tragedy of death or disappointment. It can mean separation, broken engagements or actual loss by death.

We now give you some more interpretations of the Heart Line:

IF . . . It is well defined . . . then . . .
Strong and lasting affections. Big Heartedness . . . Self-sacrifice.

IF . . . It is broken in many places . . . then . . .
Inconstancy . . . Disappointments in love . . . Disillusionment.

IF . . . It is chained . . . then . . .
Fickleness . . . Light Affections . . . Caprice . . . Flirtatiousness.

IF . . . Very thin and pale . . . then . . .
Self-love . . . Exaggerated opinion of one's own importance.

IF . . . Intercepted by many small lines . . . then . . .
Either "unlucky in love," or one who has many loves.

We have found a marked peculiarity in the difference of the Heart Line in the hand of a man, versus that of a woman. True, the emotional nature of a man will be revealed in his Heart Line, but there is something more—his ambitions toward certain ends, or his accomplishments.

If a man's Heart Line is straight across his hand, he is better suited for a type of work where he is more or less his own boss.

This is the line of the individual business or professional man.

If his Heart Line swings upward toward the first finger, then you have the executive type, either in business or in some other capacity. (This line is common among officers of the army, navy, or marine corps, either active or retired.)

If the Heart Line dips downward slightly, then you find the skilled worker in the trades, such as the machinist, electrician, or locomotive engineer.

If the Heart Line dips sharply, then the ordinary, run of the mill type of work will apply . . . the clerk, the bookkeeper, the unimportant positions in the white collar class.

If the Heart Line runs straight across the hand, with a slight up-curve and is intersected by tiny, or strong lines running toward the base of the second or first fingers (sometimes both) then he is a specialist in some type of occupation or profession . . . a man either college or university trained, or one who has gained his knowledge through practical experience, but usually following through in one single type of work. These lines going upward are often the marks of a type of work in the specialized field where a man goes forward by slow, sure steps of promotion, such as military service, government or any type where the promotion is regulated and assured.

You should never attempt to definitely designate any person's profession, or you will "put yourself on a spot." There are too many occupations and professions, each entirely different but belonging to the same general class.

For example, SCIENTIFIC may include medicine, engineering, chemistry, astronomy; CREATIVE may include writing, painting, music, advertising; EXECUTIVE may include business management, foremanship, military; TRADE may include plumbing, carpentry; PROFESSIONAL may be law, medicine, accountancy, salesmanship, athletics, etc. So, remember to place the person in the *group* in which the indications show.

Occasionally, you will see a hand so clearly indicative of a certain occupation that you can hardly miss its meaning. But, the hand does not tell what the individual may be doing, but rather what is the best vocation. We have found that in about 85% of the hands we have analyzed, the natural ability is not fitted for the occupation. Force of circumstance, lack of funds, responsibilities, the tendency to take the easiest way, puts individuals into the wrong niche in life. There is probably no finer, or greater work that a Hand Analyst can do, than to help a young man or woman find their proper place in the scheme of life, so as to have them "fit" rather than "misfit" into this pattern.

In fact, the analysis of the hands of boys and girls of high school or college age—those floundering as to what type of work to follow, is most interesting. In these cases you are trying to guide them in so far as their future is concerned. Not a future which has to do with what is usually given in "fortune telling," but a proposed Life's Highway upon which they can walk with assurance. When you see faults in these hands you should give advice as to how these should be corrected. When you see the strong points, you should stress them, in order to give confidence to help overcome the weaknesses.

Never, under any circumstances, plant the thought of inferiority or self depreciation into the mind of a young person. If you desire to use Hand Analysis in its highest form, you will employ its science carefully, and constructively . . . especially in relation to young people.

The Fate Line

The Fate Line or Line of Destiny is the next principal line. Some authorities have this line rising toward the bottom of the hand (toward the wrist) and running upward toward the fingers. However, we have found it more accurate to calculate its origin in the upper part of the palm . . . we believe it must be considered in conjunction to the Life Line, and therefore must run in the same general direction. By using this method of analysis one can obtain a far more accurate timing of important events that have happened.

Therefore, we give you according to our system, the most commonly found rising places of the Fate Line. These are: From any mount (that is the one under the fingers) . . . from the

Heart Line . . . from the Head Line . . . from the Life Line
. . . from the Center of the Palm.

In analyzing the Fate Line, you must always consider the type
of hand in which it is to be found. It is generally in the Conic,
Psychic or Philosophic Hands, and is most noticeably absent in
the Square and Spatulate Hand. It would seem from this fact that
the possessors of the Square and Spatulate Hands are of a
practical and matter-of-fact nature; that Fate, Luck or Chance,
if you please, would play but little part in their lives. In other
words, they are more or less "masters of their Fate." If, however,
the Fate Line is clear and well developed in the Square or
Spatulate Hand, you generally find evidence of success that has
been, is, or will be in their life.

We have found the Fate Line usually the indicator of success,
failure, obstacles, tragedies, changes and restrictions in life over
which the individual has little or no control—in others it indicates the regularity of the life.

The Fate Line, no matter where it starts, should run straight
and clear and extend either to the wrist, or the Mount of the
Moon. Such a line will tell of the power for good of the Line,
during the length of its course.

If the Fate Line is clear and unbroken in a hand where there is
a good Life Line, and is at some place connected to the Life Line
with another distinct line, that person has good recuperative
powers and much physical resistance to illness. He is also peculiarly protected against injury, accident and other forms of bodily
harm. We have found this type of Fate Line often in the hands of
individuals who have been close to death through different
causes, but have miraculously escaped.

However, if the Fate Line runs directly into the Life Line,
then you have something entirely different. The Fate Line running into the Life Line means that success can, or has, come into
one's life, but only through the hardest sort of work . . . no
lucky breaks have helped in anyway. When the Fate Line runs
into the Life Line in the hand of a woman, you will nearly
always find that her husband has been a ruling influence in her
life and he has attained substantial prominence directly through

his own efforts. But, if the Fate Line has a tendency to "crowd" the Life Line back toward the base of the thumb, then this success has narrowed her life considerably.

If the Fate Line rises on either the Heart or Head Line and then runs into the Life Line at a point halfway, or more than halfway up the palm, the significance is this: Restriction . . . the subject has been more or less sacrificed to the family, early environment, or some other influence which he could not set aside. This will be particularly accurate if the same marking of Fate and Life Lines are seen in both the left and right hand.

When the Fate Line starts high in the palm, under any one particular finger, the indications are possibilities of success in endeavors of an executive nature. If from the second finger, then there is usually a fairly good chance of financial independence. If from the third finger then something pertaining to the arts. If from the little finger, although this rising point is seldom seen, then success from anything of a distinctly mental nature, such as the sciences.

If the Fate Line starts very clearly at the Heart Line and goes downward deep into the Hand, one's chances for success are enhanced in proportion to the ability to use friendliness. If this Line is found in a hand where other evidences of friendliness are strongly pronounced, then it is well for that individual to always use this natural ability and be engaged in some sort of work or profession where the general public is regularly contacted.

If the Fate Line should run very deep into the Mount of the Moon, you will find a person who is quite intuitional and inspirational and should use these abilities as much as possible.

If the Fate Line runs deep into the bottom of the palm, reaching to, or almost to the wrist, then the indications are for a fairly well ordered life, particularly from a health standpoint. Such a Fate Line often is helpful to a Life Line which may appear to be short or badly disturbed through marks of illness. This type of line is unusually beneficial to younger people who may have, or have had, uncertain health in early life, because it assures better physical conditions in later years.

A Fate Line that is broken, crossed, disturbed or distorted in any way, is a positive sign of disappointments, changes, disturbances and other unfortunate experiences. By using the Life Line as your guide (according to the system of decades) you can obtain a fairly clear picture when these things happened, or may happen.

Occasionally you will find a hand, not in the classifications first given, with the Fate Line absent. This is nothing to be alarmed over, as we have found that no Fate Line is often as fine as a good Fate Line, and the interpretation should be the same.

When the Fate Line is loaded with many fine lines, some of them running upward from it, and others downward, then there is a life which will have many ups and downs in it; most of these, however, brought on by the person himself. This is especially true if such a line is found in the hand of a person who, in other markings, shows an inclination to worry.

A double Fate Line is fortunate, as it tells of a twofold career, wherein two lines of endeavor can be carried on successfully, or where Fate and Success appear to go hand in hand.

If the Fate Line breaks clearly and then begins again a little distance away from the original line, there has been a very distinct break in the life. If the Line begins to either the right or left of the original line, then this break has brought about a distinct change. The interpretation on this type of break can be given the same as the one on the breaking, or shifting Life Line (See Principal Lines Map) but in the majority of cases this break, or change, will have been brought about by something beyond the control of the individual.

If the Fate Line in a woman's hand has been broken and then you find a cross or square, close under the third or heart finger (The Sun) either touching the Head or Heart Line, you will usually find that she is a widow.

We now give you some other indications found in the condition of the Fate Line:

IF . . . The Fate Line is made up of many short lines . . .
then . . .
Indecision and fear of taking chances.

IF . . . It runs continuously but with a lot of twisting . . .
then . . .
Supersensitiveness which would interfere with success.

IF . . . Accompanied by a number of short, parallel lines
. . . then . . .
Success and life constantly being interfered with by
outside influences.

IF . . . The Fate Line branches at the beginning . . .
then . . .
Good luck and kindly Fate in early life.

IF . . . It branches distinctly into the Mount of Luna . . .
then . . .
Many changes in location . . . with possible foreign
travel.

IF . . . It branches downward toward the wrist . . . then
. . .
Better luck and kindlier Fate in the latter part of life.

IF . . . It is badly broken at the Heart Line . . . then . . .
Unfortunate friendships or love affairs.

IF . . . Very deep, long and quite straight . . . then . . .
Unusual luck, particularly in money matters, etc.

IF . . . It is very faint, but fairly well formed . . . then
. . .
Fairly good success, but much worry over conditions.

The Health Bracelet

This, as indicated in the map (Principal Lines Map) is present
in every hand and it has been proven to be a good indicator of
the general health condition.

If you find that the "Bracelet" is formed of tiny link-like
formations, you will then find a "chain of good health."

When the Bracelet is deeply cut and runs across the entire
width of the wrist, you will nearly always find a long Life Line to
compliment the good health. It has also been proven that a good
health Bracelet will support and strengthen a weak Life Line,

evidencing that, although there may have been health disturbances in childhood, or early life, the health improved in later
years.

If the Bracelet is perfectly straight across the wrist, that person
has excellent nerve control. If it curves upward toward the hand
you will find the nervous type. If there is a sort of bow-shaped
symbol formed by this bracelet, you will find the person to be the
sort to go on nervous energy, and if found on the hand of a
woman, this peculiarity indicates difficulty with childbirth. If
this bow actually breaks the bracelet, then this woman is not
likely to have children, or if she has them, her life will be
endangered by their birth.

If the Bracelet is broken in one or more places, you will also
find indications on the Life Line of a serious illness, and time of
which can be determined by the position of the break on the Life
Line.

If the Bracelet is faint and the Life Line strong, there is always
the possibility of impaired health in later life, with the recovery
slow and doubtful.

If the Bracelet does not run straight across the wrist, but
rather at an angle, and there is a disturbing line on the Head
Line, you will often find there has been some serious nervous
disorder, such as a collapse, or nervous breakdown.

Marriage Lines or Lines of Emotional Attachment

Probably the Marriage Lines create more interest then all the
other lines in the hand. There seems to be a peculiar fascination
about these which invariably bring inquiries about them.

Many Palmists, and books on Palmistry, state that the number
of marriage lines in the hand denote the number of marriages,
either in the past, or as related to the future. We take an absolute
and irrevocable stand against any such statements and our years
of experience and intense study of these lines have proven us
right.

In the first place, the Hand does not recognize marriage in its
true sense. Marriage is, according to Webster, "the act of legally

uniting a man and woman in wedlock through a marriage ceremony." Marriage is an institution established by the church and state and does not always represent emotion.

But, first let us locate the most fascinating and much discussed lines. They are to be found on the inside portion of the hand, lying between the base of the little finger and above the Heart Line. By clenching the hand these lines will be brought out plainly, but you should never consider these while the hand is in this position, but rather when it is relaxed.

These lines run parallel to the Heart Line and are usually in relation to the intensity, depth and strength of the Heart Line. Therefore, again our contention that these cannot be said to be true Marriage Lines, but those of emotion (an emotion which ordinarily is to be considered as related to attachments with the opposite sex) yet we have seen them relate to other emotions as well—toward family, father, mother, children or friends.

Here is the primary and most important indication of a "Marriage Line." Work from this, as your basic idea and you will never be far wrong on any interpretation, no matter what it may be: If there are one, or more of these "Marriage Lines" deep and well defined and supported by a good Heart Line, you have the indication of a person capable of strong, sincere affection and lasting friendship. This type of line, when a marriage has occured, invariably shows that it has been successful in every way. If the lines are very faint, then you will have the reverse, depending of course, upon the intensity of the Heart Line. The stronger the Heart Line, the more power is given to the "Marriage Line" and conversely, the weaker or more disturbed the Heart Line, the less power and importance.

If you see one, deep, strong, long Marriage Line, with a good Heart Line supported by a good Head Line, then you will know these truths to be self-evident . . . a person who can be trusted implicitly in emotions, friendships, loyalty, etc., even though this person has never married, or may never do so.

So, again we say, do not always take these lines to mean marriage alone. If you do, you may find yourself wrong as many times as you are right.

These lines do have a peculiar bearing upon the relations with the opposite sex. Being primarily emotional lines, with emotions pertaining to affection (usually associated with affairs of the heart or romance) they are therefore indicative of emotional attachments, although these attachments may never result in marriage.

When analyzing these lines as relating to heart emotions, engagements, attachments, marriage, etc., remember this line is the mark of an attachment. We have found on the hands of more serious types of individuals, that engagements and love affairs which have been broken, will register the same as the actual marriage would—sometimes these lines are even stronger.

In the sector where the "Marriage Lines" lie which we will call the "House of Emotion," or "The House of Marriage," you will find a fairly definite time indicator as to the age when various emotional affairs (or marriage) took place. As we said before, "The House of Emotion" lies in a space bounded by the Heart Line at its bottom and the base of the little finger at the top. The center of this section represents the 25th year, so if the marriage line lies in this position, marriage, or a deep attachment occurred at approximately that age. If it lies below the center, the marriage or a deep attachment, occurred earlier. If it lies close to the Heart Line, then the age of the attachment is usually below twenty.

If these lines lie closer to the base of the little finger, then the emotional nature was not expressed until late in life.

If you definitely know a person is married, you can estimate quite closely the age of that marriage by looking at the first line up from the Heart Line and calculating that against that person's present age.

If the line lies in a position which would place it beyond the present age, then there would be every indication that marriage has not yet taken place.

But, we cannot stress this point too strongly, you cannot at any time, or under any circumstance, predict a marriage that has not been consummated. Neither can you tell a person who is already married that there is another marriage in store. In our opinion, this is one of the most cruel and thoughtless things any palm analyst can do, although it is constantly practised.

Individual after individual has told us that some one who is supposed to be an authority on the subject has predicted more than one marriage. Before you commit yourself to such a statement think what such a statement may mean to a person who is happily married; in order for another marriage to take place, the present happy one must be broken, either through death or divorce.

The rank and file of people may ask these things lightly and say: "How many times am I to marry?" This is said in a spirit of jest, but when a palmist says seriously: "Twice or three times," there is bound to be a subconscious reaction. This is intensified in proportion to the accuracy of the palmist in other facts pertaining to the past and the impressionability of the individual.

Many, many times we have had women ask us this question: "Will I be married more than once?" and then add: . . . "Please tell me the truth." When we have carefully explained that these so-called "Marriage Lines" cannot definitely predict anything in reference to future marriage, there has always been a great relief. Remember, palm analysis is not intended to implant improper subconscious thoughts in any one. Its purpose is to assist and help . . . not to tear down and hinder. Therefore, be truthful about these Marriage Lines, as well as all other Lines in the hand. You may disappoint some who want their "fortunes told," but with the great majority you will find yourself gaining respect and admiration for your frankness.

Now let us go back to the subject of the "Marriage Lines." Remember, the first line up from the Heart Line, is to be considered as the indicator of marriage, or heart attachment taking place early in life. Therefore, first study these lines carefully in the hands of those whom you definitely know to be married, or have been married, in order to perfect yourself in the art of determining time.

If one of these lines on the hand of one into whose life marriage has come, shows a disturbance, you will usually have a definite indication as to the effect upon the marriage.

We have found a true Marriage Line crossed out with a line cutting over it near the inside end, to mean a marriage broken by death. If there is a fork at the same end, then marriage has been broken by separation or divorce. These same marks, particularly the latter one, will often represent a strong love affair, or broken engagement.

If the true Marriage Line is disturbed by a number of cross lines cutting over its entire length, you generally find some discord in the existing marriage. This does not always mean trouble in the accepted sense of the word, but will often represent worry from a financial angle, or illness on the part of the marriage partner.

If, when the true Marriage Line is found, there is a parallel line and both of these either join at the end in order to form a distinct fork, or if they are tied together by a connecting line, then you generally have a marriage that is going quite smoothly. This is especially true when the lines are clear and deep.

In the hand of a widow, you will many times find the crossed out Marriage Line and then a cross lying either near the Head, or Heart Line, and under, or near the third, or ring finger. This combination is almost a certain sign of the death of the husband.

If the true Marriage Line dips downward toward the Heart Line, you can nearly always count on this marriage being a case of "love at first sight." This marriage was prompted by strong emotional attachment on both sides.

If the Line sweeps upward toward the little finger, the courtship was probably rather long and protracted with the possibility of many obstacles in the way of ultimate marriage.

We have proven the foregoing facts, time and again. Everything else in the course of our experiments has proven to be erroneous and merely a matter of conjecture. So you can see from these indications how little can actually be told from the so-called "Marriage Lines."

Therefore we say again . . . we hope you will be extremely careful in what you say in reference to them. The reading of these lines is as ticklish a piece of business as is the reading of the Life Line in making any definite statements in reference to illness and expectancy of life.

The Career Line

This Line is very odd but extremely important, as it is the index to a career, either as to the possibility of one to come, the existence of a career and the promise of success, or changes in the career.

The Life Line, Fate Line and Career Line have much in common. In fact, one could almost call the Career Line the "Second Life Line." Although it shows no indication of health, illness or sudden changes in the general or specific ways of life, it does point out clearly the way of occupation, whether this be in a woman's hand, that of a wife, mother or general supervisor of the home. Or in a man's hand it indicates high honors and other rewards obtained through profession, politics, business, arts, sciences, etc.

The Career Line usually originates between the third and little finger, or beneath either of these two fingers, and runs toward the wrist . . . (See Principal Map Lines)

The Career Line is often quite distinct in its entirety, or there are segments of it to be found in the left hand. If the Career Line is perfectly straight, unbroken and good in the Left Hand, the significance is usually that a Career was definitely decided upon in early life. If the Career Line follows through in the same manner in the right hand, that Career, as a rule, has been followed.

If the Career Line is faint, distorted or disjointed in the left hand, then there were ideas of a certain career in early life, but through one cause or another, this was never followed through. You will invariably find this type of Career Line in the hands of young people who have not decided definitely upon a career.

When the Career Line runs into the Life Line, then the Career has more or less been chosen by decision (not necessarily meaning that the original plan was carried out) and that the selection of the Career was not a hit and miss affair. If the Career Line starts at, or crosses the Fate Line, then Fate, Luck, Chance and

Circumstance played a prominent part in determining the career. This oftentimes indicates where the easiest way was taken, or where the career being followed, came unexpectedly.

You will often find sharp breaks in the Career Line. These invariably show shifts in the Career. If these breaks are clean cut and fairly well apart, then the change has been from one field to another. If these breaks are very close together, and there is very little distortion on the Career Line, then changes may have been or are coming in the person's life, but the general Career will be the same.

Occasionally you will find two Career Lines running parallel. This symbolizes two careers . . . possibly one a vocation, the other an avocation or hobby. Such lines are to be seen quite often in hands which denote versatility, where there must be some interest aside from the usual work-a-day occupation. A man with this double career line may be actually following two careers, or he may have in addition to his work, or profession, some other interest . . . such as music, art, collecting stamps, photography, clubs, lodges, etc.

In a woman's hand these double Career Lines often show where marriage and a definite career go hand in hand. In other words, she "can carry water on both shoulders." These strong double Career Lines in a woman's hand do not necessarily mean that she works at something because she is compelled to do so from a financial standpoint, but because it is her desire. She wants "more than one iron in the fire." These double Career Lines in a woman's hand have even a stronger meaning when either one or both cross the Heart Line. Of course, these lines can mean the same in a man's hand, in reference to hobbies, etc. But it will always raise a woman above being just an ordinary housekeeper, or a person who merely wastes time, even though her husband is in a good financial position.

If the Career Line has distinct branches toward other fingers, except the fourth (the career finger), the career, in a general way, is colored by what these fingers represent . . . the third finger means a career through public contact . . . the second finger a career of unusual financial importance. It is seldom that there are any branches running toward the first finger.

We give you fair warning . . . the Career Lines are very difficult to decipher . . . however, they are of such vital importance to the hand analysis, that much study should be given to them.

6

THE LESSER LINES

As previously stated, there are Seven Principal Lines which have been located and described. We now come to the second set of lines . . . the Seven Lesser Lines (See Maps Although the Lesser Lines are in reality not as important as the Principal Lines, they have a definite place in Hand Analysis. It is really not important how these Seven Lesser Lines are classified in regard to importance, as you will probably analyze these in the order in which you notice them. However, for a semblance of order, we will list them as follows:

No. 1—The Financial Line. No. 2—The Sun Line. No. 3—The Children. No. 4—Travel Lines. No. 5—Line of Intuition. (These five are shown on Map of Lesser Lines.) No. 6.—The Line of Protection. (See Maps.) No. 7—The Girdle of Venus. (See Maps)

The order in which these Seven Lesser Lines are listed is in ratio to frequency of appearance. It is seldom you will find the last three.

In the thousands of hands we have analyzed, we have yet to find all 14 lines. In fact, it is quite a thrill to find more than seven lines in any hand which is made possible by grouping lines from the first and second sections . . . the Principal and Lesser Lines.

It will not take you long to realize that the analysis of the

Lines of the hand is not such a formidable task; not as much as if all fourteen lines were to be seen in every hand.

In considering the Lesser Lines, treat them as you did the Principal Lines. That is . . . take into consideration depth, color, straightness, length, etc.

And now to the explanation of the second set of Lines in the Hand . . . The Lesser Lines.

In the Handprint of Lesser Lines (Fig. 6-1), you see five of the Lesser Lines. These are: No. 1—Financial Line. No. 2.— Sun Line. No. 3—Lines of the Children. No. 4—Travel Lines. No. 5—Line of Intuition. The Lines of Children (No. 3) and Health Bracelet have been drawn and blended into the Hand Print, as it is impossible to get a good impression of the entire hand and wrist simultaneously.

Briefly, the actual history of this hand is as follows: The lady is financially independent, in fact wealthy, through two sources . . . inheritance from her own family, and through her husband's estate; single, straight Fate Line starting at Base of Second Finger (No. 1); her late husband was nationally prominent (No. 2 Long Sun Line); she has two children (No. 3); she is naturally intuitive and imaginative (No. 5) using these attributes in a creative way. This lady has traveled extensively, both by land and sea, having spent much time in foreign lands (Travel Lines No. 4, many and varied).

In this hand we also see very excellent proof of the presence of letters, or initials (explained on page 148) which are prominent in her life. Notice the letter "W" twice. Once under the second finger; once under the third finger. The first "W" is the initial letter of her maiden name, from whence came the inheritance. The second "W" is the first letter of her married name. Beneath the Heart Line a perfect "H," her daughter's first initial.

The major lines converge and form two letters near the base of the palm, the letters "M" and "A" intertwined. "M" is the initial of the lady's first name, one traditional in the family, carried by mother, grandmother and great-grandmother. The "A" the first letter of her father's Christian name. In these letters appearing so strongly, you have an outstanding example of strong family love and influence.

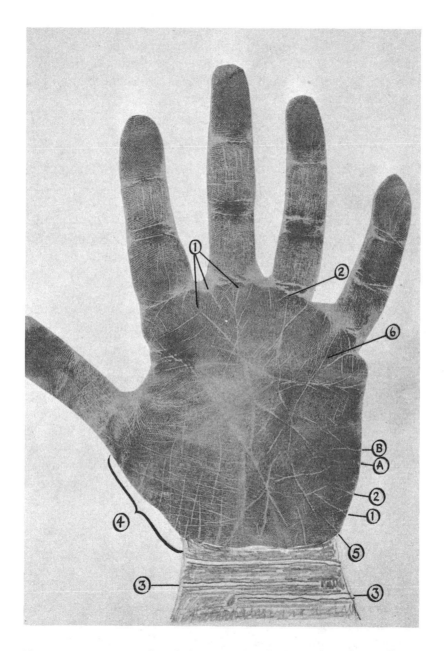

Fig. 6-1. A woman's hand showing clearly four of the lesser lines.

Study the general composition of this hand. It shows practicability coupled with originality and imagination. Much generosity and philanthropy are also shown. (Wide space between fingers and strong, upsweeping Heart Line.) Firmness and leadership is indicated by the long, well set thumb. She is interested and is a leader of national note in practical charity.

The Financial Lines

These invariably lie under the second finger, which is logical, as the second finger is OBJECTIVITY and certainly financial security and material gain are a definite objective.

You will find these lines in many peculiar positions—sometimes running obliquely, but most of the time perpendicularly under the second finger. Occasionally these are free of the Heart Line, but most often there is a direct or indirect joining of the two. There is an old saying that seems to hold true in this instance . . . "After the affairs of the heart, or romance, comes the affairs of finance." Hence the close proximity to the Heart Line.

First, the most common type of Financial Line: It rises straight up toward the base of the second finger and is fairly clear and fairly deep (Lesser Lines Number One). This indicates financial security in the life . . . not wealth, but a sufficient amount of money, either through work, or other revenue to promise financial independence. This type of line is quite common in the hand of an individual who may hold a position which is secure, and also carries some sort of pension in old age. Government people, teachers, police or firemen, railroad employees of certain types have this line.

In the hands of a married woman, who is entirely dependent upon her husband for her support, this line indicates steadiness in the husband's position, especially if it starts from the Heart Line.

If there are several lines in the Financial Sector (beneath the 2nd finger), then the indication is not so good, as there is evidence of financial upsets and worries, either in the past, or the present. However, if one strong line appears in this group, and there is a fork at the bottom of the Life Line, then the promise is for better financial conditions as the years go on, and security in one way or another in old age.

If the Financial Lines are crossed by another Line, there have been Financial Reverses of a disastrous nature. However, if the Lines continue and are just crossed, not broken, that person has risen, or will rise again from these financial losses and regain much of the lost ground.

In a woman's hand, if the Financial Lines go down through the Heart Line to the Life Line, you will usually find that she is self-supporting.

If there are two lines in a woman's hand, each as strong as the other, you will generally find two sources of income in the family; that of her husband and her own. Occasionally, you will see one line being stronger, which quite often indicates that the wife's income is larger than that of the husband's.

If the Financial Line branches upward having many off-shoots like the branch of a tree, then the indications of a continual branching out financially are present. This will show in the hands of both men and women. If found in the hand of a married woman who is dependent upon her husband for support, it shows his financial progress. If her own Career Line is prominent, then it indicates her financial progress.

If a line, or suggestion of a line, cuts across the hand from under the third finger, toward the financial group, you will find financial loss has been occasioned through deceit, fraud, etc.— from friends, those trusted, or through the marriage partner. This has been expressly true in cases where elderly men and women have lost much money through late marriages.

In connection with the Financial Line, you must learn about the "Line of Unearned Money" which is startling in its accuracy. This line is so designated because it refers to money which does not come through the regular channels of income. It is the continuation of the Fate Line up into the Financial Sector (see Line No. 1 Lesser Line Map). Here is a specific instance where inheritance played an important part in financial gain. It has been found in the hands of men and women who have won money in the sweepstakes, contests, received annuities, returns on investments, through bonuses, etc.

The Sun Line

The Sun Line is often considered to be a support of the Fate Line, and we have found such to be the case. If the Sun Line and Fate Line are both present and good, then that person is indeed fortunate as Life and Fate should be quite kind.

The Sun Line is also looked upon by many exponents to mean distinction and fame. We would rather take the Sun Line as the indicator of cheerfulness and a sunny disposition, because we have found those possessing the Sun Line are usually optimistic people.

We have always read the Sun Line in accordance with the run of the Life Line (the same as mentioned in connection with the Fate Line) and therefore consider the rising point in the upper part of the palm (beneath the fingers) rather than from the base of the palm.

It will rise directly under the third finger and close to the base of the finger. Directly under the third finger, but actually starting at the Heart Line; directly under the third finger, and at the Head Line; directly under the third finger and below the Head Line.

If the Sun Line starts above the Heart Line and runs either into the Head Line or into the Mount of the Moon, then it is correct in length. This type of Sun Line represents much laughter, joy, optimism and happiness brought about by the person's own cheerful attitude toward life. These individuals will not be of the fretful, worrying type, but rather the sort who believes, "sufficient for the day is the evil thereof . . . let tomorrow take care of itself." They usually have an excellent sense of humor, see the funny side of everything and always make the best of any bad situation. They are naturally friendly and attract others to them by their kindliness and spirit of fun. Most persons with this type Sun Line are natural wits and are constantly using this talent to good advantage. They just naturally like people and should be in some line of activity where they contact the general public. They are usually fond of animals and have a great love for children.

If the Sun Line, rising as just mentioned, runs into the Mount of the Moon, then the indication is that of a person who has a very fertile imagination and this talent can be used to good advantage in any form of activity where the creative is necessary. This is particularly true of any line of endeavor connected with the arts.

If the Sun Line is long and there is a long third finger, and a sloping Head Line, you have a person who will take chances. This is the mark of "the gambler," not necessarily in the accepted sense of the word where dollars and cents are involved, but rather, the person who believes in the old adage . . . "Nothing ventured, nothing gained." Peculiarly enough these people are generally quite fortunate in acting upon this idea and will be more successful in life by doing so.

A STAR on the Sun Line is always a good mark, and if other lines in the hand are favorable, usually tells of success in life.

When both the Fate and Sun Lines are plainly marked and both good, the evidence is almost always for success in life . . . if not in worldly things, then in good friendships, a lot of fun out of living and an existence that as a whole is good. We have found these lines very often in the hands of older people, who according to accepted standards have never attained much in money and other material things, but have a great amount of pleasure being just themselves. Happy, cheerful people who have delighted in doing good, and in the final analysis, we believe this to be one of the highest attainments in life.

The Sun Line is not often seen, so when you see it, study it carefully because its possession is fortunate. There is one thing certain about the possessor of the Sun Line . . . these individuals will not be pessimists, just the opposite, and as a result a pleasant person to know and contact.

Lines of Children

These lines are among the most interesting to be found in the hand, and create as much curiosity as do the "Marriage Lines." The Lines of Children are excellent as "testers" to those who are skeptical of the truths to be revealed in the hands. If these lines are read accurately, and they can be, you will impress and at the same time inspire confidence in other parts of your analysis.

Heretofore, the Lines of the Children have usually been located in "The House of Marriage." You will see evidence of this fact quite often when mentioning the "children." Notice that the subject will immediately double the fist and turn the "House of Marriage" upward and toward you. These Lines of Children in "The House of Marriage" are claimed to show in this manner . . . fine perpendicular lines running downward from the Marriage Line to the Heart Line. Others claim that these come from the base of the little finger toward the Marriage Line. We have found no accuracy in either of these instances. In the first place, there are often myriads of lines in the House of Marriage, which as we explained before, indicate some sort of trouble in domestic affairs. We felt, ever since we took up the study of Hand Analysis, that there must be some place in the Hand where more clarity and accuracy could be found than in the "House of Marriage." After long study, we found it—in the wrist.

We explained in the Chapter devoted to "The Bracelets" the significance of these toward children and childbirth, barrenness and fertility. This was the first fact we learned which gave us the clue for using the wrist to determine the Children.

So, again we discarded old methods of Hand Analysis and Palmistry and now use the wrist to determine the children, or interest in children in a person's life.

The Lines of the Children lie directly below the Bracelet. (See Map of Lesser Lines.) You should generally use the right wrist, but occasionally you will have to use both wrists. Sometimes you may have a bit of difficulty in locating these lines in a wrist which is very plump, or one which is scrawny, but under ordinary circumstances, you can read them quite accurately after practice. We have found the best way to bring these lines into view, is to tilt the hand backward toward the wrist, then allow it to return to normal position and sight along the wrist toward the elbow. You read these lines (aside from the bracelet) which stand out most prominently.

The lines to be considered are the ones which either completely cross the wrist unbroken, or that go at least two thirds of the distance. Lines of this type nearly always indicate the living children.

Short, or broken lines, often represent the ones which are dead, either having lived only a short time in infancy, or where there was conception, but no natural birth. There is no way that we have discovered so far to tell the death of children who have reached maturity in the true Children's Lines. These indications are to be found in other parts of the hand . . . the cross, squares and other malefic disturbances.

Sometimes, but not every time, you can distinguish the difference in the sex of the children. The easiest way to tell is in the difference of the depth and length of the lines; the most powerful lines show boys and the lesser lines girls. But strong and weak lines can mean something else—the indication of the children who had the best health in babyhood and childhood, and vice versa. So this may come under the classification of a "guess," and we do not believe that "guessing" has any place in Scientific Hand Analysis, because there are too many definite facts which may be established to necessitate conjecture.

As we said before, you will generally find all the children on the right wrist, but it is well to look at the left one also. For example, you may mention that you find two lines on the right wrist. The person will say there are more. Then by looking at the left wrist, you will nearly always see the others. We found much accuracy in determining sex when the Lines of Children are in both wrists, but we do not recommend this method for positiveness.

In order to determine the possibility of future children, follow the same method just given, but you will notice the lines will be very short and indistinct. It is not wise to make a positive statement in reference to expectancy on children, but rather say, "Here is a possibility," or words to that effect.

Now for another peculiar phase of the Lines of the Children. These are to be applied in the same general manner as the Emotional Lines (Marriage Lines). We explained quite carefully about these Lines not representing actual marriage; so with the Lines of Children. These would not always indicate a woman's own children . . . her own flesh and blood. They can just as well show interest in a certain number of children . . . younger brothers and sisters, nieces, nephews, adopted children, stepchildren, etc.

To illustrate this point, here is an example: At one time we saw five distinct marks of children in the wrist of a middle-aged woman, who had never married. But this, in brief, was her story . . . her sister and brother-in-law were killed; she took over the raising of the children and later adopted them as her own.

It goes without saying, that you must use tact when dealing with the Children's Lines. Do not blurt out the fact that a person has children until you are reasonably certain that there is, or has been a marriage. If you are in doubt the best way to save yourself embarrassment is to mention the "influence of children." By doing this, you are not only protecting yourself, but at the same time giving the really correct interpretation of these lines.

Another interesting thing we have discovered is that the Lines of Children will sometimes be as prominent in a man's hand as in a woman's. This fact may mean identically the same as it does with a woman . . . interest in children, fatherhood, children in his life, etc. It is astonishing to see how often there are the same number of lines in a husband's wrist as there are in that of his wife's. There is another interesting thing in this connection . . . a husband who shows the lines of his children very plainly is a good father, having the interest of his children at heart and attempting to discharge his duties to them in the best possible manner.

Indication of twins can often be seen in the Lines of the

Children. These are usually shown in two very distinct lines all the way across the hand and very close together—sometimes not touching, sometimes intertwined. If one of these lines is clearly broken, then the strong possibility exists that one of the twins did not live.

We have also found out that when the Line of the Children is very plain, you can closely estimate how soon after marriage the first child was born, and if there were more, about how far apart these arrived. The starting point for this calculation is taken at the bracelet. The closer the first Line of Children lies to this Bracelet, the earlier the birth. However, this analysis is rather difficult and can only be arrived at through careful study, experimentation and practice.

Travel Lines

Again on the Travel Lines, we are at variance with some of the accepted locations as given by most writers on palm analysis. Nearly all give these as located in the Mount of the Moon, near the base of the palm (See Fig. 6-1). We have found these to be fairly accurate in regard to foreign travel, but not so when it comes to ordinary travel.

We have found the Travel Lines located on the Mount of Venus, in that section which is inside of the Life Line and toward the thumb. Of course, in reality these are the "Action Lines" (which will be explained later), but Travel Lines appear here as well. These can usually be distinguished when they are heavy, clearly defined and seldom, if ever, cross the Life Line. The longer and heavier these lines are, the longer are the trips . . . short heavy lines denote the shorter trips.

This system has been proven accurate in analyzing hands of people from every walk of life. Many of these people living in small towns in the mid-western part of the country had no lines in this particular sector and we found, by investigation, that these individuals had in most instances, not traveled beyond the confines of their native state; many, in fact, had not been 100 miles from their original homes.

As the opposite example, our contacts in Washington brought us in touch with hundreds of army and navy people, both men and women, and in their hands were found profuse lines in the travel sector. In some instances these lines were so definitely marked that we were able to tell exactly how many changes of location had been made.

By using the decade system, as applied to the Life Line, you can determine by a person's age and by counting ahead, or backward, whether or not the travel has been, is to come, or both.

After analyzing this travel sector, look at the extreme base of the Mount of Venus. There you will usually find more or less lines. These nearly always represent long trips . . . trips of a thousand miles or more. However, you cannot, distinguish the past from the future with these lines, so you have to treat them as indicating long trips that will be taken during the course of a life.

We have found one outstanding peculiarity in this set of lines: If there is a heavy line, or several heavy lines rather close together in this sector at the base of the hand, lying very close to the thumb, then that person has done some travel by air, or will certainly do so in the future. Almost without exception we have found these lines in the hands of those connected with aviation such as military fliers, pilots, navigators, stewardesses, etc.

Strong, straight lines cutting across in the first named travel sector, usually indicate long trips taken from one extreme part of the country to the other. We call these lines the "Lines of the Opposite," as we have also found them to indicate that individuals possessing them, live in opposite parts of the country. This has been especially true in Washington, where the government workers come from distant parts of the country.

The Travel Lines are most fascinating, and their study is recommended because nearly everyone is interested in the possibility of travel in life, and those who have done considerable traveling are proud of the fact. Therefore, if you can be accurate on the analysis of past travel, you have another point to help you to establish your correctness in reading a hand.

Line of Intuition

The Complete Intuition Line is one rarely seen in a hand. You will occasionally find a suggestion of it, but seldom see it clearly marked. It usually starts at some point fairly well over to the inside of the hand on the Mount of the Moon, and runs in a semi-circle upward toward the little finger. This line, to be true, should not start from any line, but should run through the Heart and Head Line and stop a short distance away from the base of the Little Finger, on the Mount of Mercury. (See Map Lesser Lines No. 2.)

If the Intuition Line is plainly marked as described, then you have a person possessing a great amount of intuitive ability, to the point of being highly impressionistic. These people generally possess some psychic power and have the peculiar faculty of "feeling in their bones that something is going to happen"—and it generally does. If the Head and the Life Line are well separated and both of these are quite a distance away from the Heart Line, then that person should follow his "Intuition and Hunches" to the full extent. He will be far better in doing so, than trying to think a thing out to a logical conclusion. This ability is more pronounced if all the fingers, including the thumb, can be easily bent backward at the first joints.

As we said before, the Intuition Line is seldom found to be perfect. Therefore, if segments of it are found, you must judge a person's intuitive ability by the strength, length and condition of the line. Those without any trace of this line are usually rather devoid of the intuitive power and should not depend very much upon their "first impressions."

If the Intuitive Line is clearly marked, but there is a sharp joining at the Life and Head Lines, then you have one who has the ability, but is afraid to use it. If the Line is not very well formed, but has the wide open spaces between the Head and Life Line, then that person will generally use what intuitive power he may possess to good advantage and may learn to develop it to such a point that he can depend upon it to quite a degree.

Line of Protection

This Line runs inside of the Life Line between it and the thumb. It is sometimes called "The Second Life Line," and in this name you have the best explanation of its significance, as it is generally found in the hand of a person who has in reality been "protected" against accidents, bodily injury, etc. In other words, it seems to have a peculiar significance of denoting one with almost a charmed life.

It also strengthens and adds to the power of the Life Line. Therefore, if this Line of Protection is found in a hand, even though the Life Line does not appear to be good, your interpretation can be that the Life Line is in reality better than it appears.

We have also found this "Line of Protection" in the hands of many persons, women more often than men, who have had a "protected life." These are the type who have been sheltered in the home surroundings, never having to worry about their "board and keep," and have often been given many advantages by their parents. They then married rather young to men who have also sheltered them. However, such a line is not overly good as it is generally found in the hand of a person who has little importance in life. Things have usually been too easy, with the result that "life's real adventure has passed them by."

The "Protection Line" often runs the full length of the Life Line . . . and sometimes is seen only in a segment. If the former, then the significance is protection and easy going through the life. If the latter, you will nearly always find that over a period (generally estimated by the decade system) there have been periods of danger, either from illness, or peril which have been overcome through almost miraculous conditions.

If the Protection Line is of considerable length and the Fate Line and Life Line are joined at some place in the hand, then you have a person who is, has been, and will be, lucky in nearly every phase of Life. The Protection Line, by the way, is seldom seen. We have found it once in about every 1,000 hands. Therefore, from this fact you can get a good idea of its true significance.

Of all the Hand Prints we have in our possession, the one on Lesser Lines (No. 3) best illustrates the Line of Protection (No. 1). We have also in combination with this Line another . . . The Line of Restriction (No. 2).

Now let us see how accurately these two lines connect with the past life of this woman. She was raised in an orphanage, having no knowledge of her family. (Note complete absence of family lines No. 3.) The complete break in the Fate Line, above the Head Line, shows the unkindness of Fate because of the lack of parents. The short line dropping from the Head Line (a continuation of the Fate Line) and connecting with the Life Line, becomes the Line of Restriction, because of the early discipline and control of an institution.

However, the Line of Protection played a prominent part in her life. First, she was afforded "protection," shelter and education through the institution. And, strange as it seems, there were three times in her life, between the ages of seven and twenty-one, when she miraculously escaped death. (Note three lines crossing the Line of Protection) (No. 4) but all stopping at the Life Line.

Notice the perfect squareness of this palm, with the strong, firm, thin hand. Notice also the medium long, round tipped fingers. This woman rose above her "restrictions," making a definite place for herself in the profession she chose . . . nursing. Square for practicability, well padded for sympathy, round-tipped fingers for doing things well. With a minimum of lines there is a well balanced nervous and physical makeup.

It is unfortunate that the Career Line does not show more clearly in this print. Segments of it can be seen rising from the Life Line and again under the fourth finger. This woman has been a nurse for almost forty years and is now superintendent of a large, nationally known public institution, and considered to be outstanding in her field.

The Girdle of Venus

This Line (Lesser Lines No. 4) is the rarest of all Lines in the hand. It will only show up clearly once in ten thousand hands. There are many opinions concerning the Girdle, but we have found it to be really a mark of genius. If it is clear, well defined, unbroken, and runs in almost a perfect semicircle, between the first and second finger to a point between the third and little finger, you have a person who has a tremendous natural ability in one form or another. This talent is generally leaning toward art, music, literature and the more aesthetic things in life, rather than the prosaic and practical.

Even if the line is good, it does not do much to help the general temperament because those who have it are nearly always temperamental, changeable and restless. If the hand is strong, the Head Line and thumb strong, there is a better condition than if these were weak.

If the Girdle is broken, chained or otherwise badly disturbed, then you will find a person very high strung, nervous and often highly irritable. This type will always be seeking changes of various sorts. He will be, to a great extent, "a jack of all trades and master of none."

If that portion of the Girdle which lies in the vicinity of the third finger, has lines which run into the Heart Line, or into the so-called Marriage Lines, then there is often danger of unreasoning and extreme jealousy which often ruins love, friendships and marriage. The significance of this type of Girdle is intensified when found upon a Psychic or Conic Hand. Peculiarly, but naturally, you seldom find the Girdle upon the Square or Spatulate Hand, but nearly always, on the Conic or Psychic Hand.

The lady whose hand imprint we have selected to illustrate the Girdle of Venus (Fig. 6-2) is truly representative of its meaning and influence. She is talented in many lines . . . music, both vocal and instrumental. (Now a teacher of both.) Music is her main talent, in which she has been very successful, but, she also

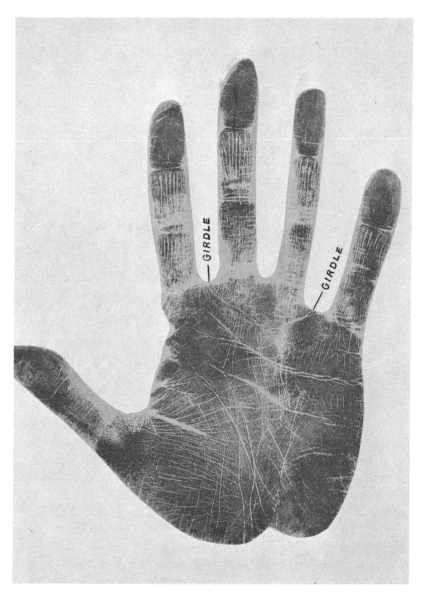

Fig. 6-2. Lesser lines number 4.

has dramatic ability, paints and does interior decorating as a hobby.

In other sections of her hand you see marks of her talent. Note the wide outswing of the palm, under the first finger . . . always an indication of creative ability. See the long, but round-tipped fingers . . . artistic, but also capable of doing things of an artistic nature in a practical way.

Then there is the low swinging Head Line, with many branches dropping to the Mount of the Moon . . . imagination.

Her Career Line is very straight and quite long, showing that her career was started early, has been progressive and is still continuing.

Many Travel Lines are shown as travel has been quite important and necessary in her profession in the entertainment field.

There is also a good Sun Line, indicating prominence and success in life, in this instance through her own efforts. Note the Sun Line and the Career Line joining near the left side of the base of the palm.

7

THE MOUNTS

After analyzing the other parts of the hand in the rotation in which these have been presented, we next come to: The Mounts.

These are the high spots, or bumps under the fingers and sometimes around the edges of the hand which have the unfortunate habit of picking up blisters and callouses from unfamiliar manual labor. However, despite the fact that we may swear at these when a beautiful crop of sore spots develop after an unaccustomed session with the lawn-mower, hammer or oars of a boat, these play an important part in the story of the hand.

Before going into the study of the Mounts, fix this one fact in your mind: Their prominence effects . . . lack of prominence detracts. Also one highly pronounced Mount may pull your Life out of kilter, or the reverse.

First it is well to commit to memory the names of the Mounts. They are, as follows: Under the index finger . . . The Mount of Jupiter. Under the second finger . . . The Mount of Saturn. Under the third finger . . . The Mount of the Sun. Under the little finger . . . The Mount of Mercury. That portion of the hand between the thumb and the Life Line . . . The Mount of Venus. That portion of the inside of the hand between the Head Line and the base of the palm . . . The Mount of the Moon. Directly above the Mount of the Moon, between the Head and Heart Lines . . . The Mount of Mars. On the outer edge of the palm directly above the Mount of Venus and below the Head Line . . . again the Mount of Mars. Study the Map until you are entirely familiar with the location and names of the Mounts.

Very seldom will you find any, or all of the Mounts relating to the fingers in their proper places . . . directly at the root or base of the finger. These are mostly found leaning toward a neighboring Mount, or finger. You will be able to determine the significance of such leanings once you have mastered the interpretation of the mount in its proper place.

Lines and marks, touching upon, or crossing each Mount, will often add to or detract from their significance. These indications will be explained as we go along.

The Mount of Jupiter

No Mount under the index finger or Jupiter, means that the subject is somewhat lacking in self-respect and ambition.

When this Mount is fairly well developed, you have a person who has ambition and pride, one who is generally honorable in his dealings with others and possesses a great amount of enthusiasm. This is especially true of a man's Mount.

If the Mount of Jupiter is in excess, then a domineering spirit, dictatorial attitude toward others, and an inclination toward extreme selfishness is indicated.

The Mount of Saturn

It is seldom that a pronounced Mount will be found under the second finger, or Saturn, as this is the mark of the "lone wolf," and fortunately for the world, there are few individuals of this type. As a rule most hands are almost entirely void of this Mount.

If, however, you find it fairly well developed, you have a person who loves solitude and as a result is not sociable. He is nearly always quiet and studious with a flair for the things rather unusual, such as mysticism, the occult and other out-of-the-ordinary pursuits. Confirmed bachelors often show evidence of the Mount of Saturn.

If it is highly developed, then there is a tendency to a gloomy, morose nature. If the Mount of the Moon is so highly developed as to be immediately noticeable, with a sharply sloping Head Line, then many fancied slights or wrongs with a leaning to melancholy are indicated.

The Mount of the Sun

When this Mount, under the third finger, or Sun, is well developed, you have a very cheerful and optimistic outlook on life, with a love for all things that are beautiful and artistic. This is also the mark of the very friendly person, particularly if there is a well developed Mount of Venus. Strangely enough, this type of Mount indicates friendliness, but the possessor, through some irony of fate, will nearly always have difficulties with friends and loved ones. This Mount when well developed also is a clear indicator of some artistic talent, usually music.

If the Mount of the Sun is in excess, then the indications are toward unusual vanity, self-praise and a desire for show and pretense.

The Mount of Mercury

The absence of this Mount, under the little finger, tells of a person who does not possess powers of leadership or close application . . . the sign of a poor businessman.

When fairly well developed, there are two definite meanings, either favorable or unfavorable, depending upon the type of hand. If on a good hand, otherwise well marked, there will be business ability, power of expression and often a desire for the sciences. If the Head Line is straight, then an excellent lawyer, as it gives force and clarity in reasoning; if the Head Line is slightly curved downward, one who is not afraid of the hardest kind of physical work, but usually of the mental type; if the Mount is well developed in a hand where there is a broken Head Line, then one who is too nervous and restless for any fixed purpose; if the Heart Line is disturbed, then you often have a wanderer who lives by luck and chance.

If the Mount of Mercury is in excess, you have a person who is cunning at heart. He may not show it openly, but he is usually trying to get the best of the other person in one way, or another.

The Mount of Venus

This is the feminine Mount, the same as the Mount of Jupiter was the masculine Mount.

Its absence denotes a cold nature, one who is hard-hearted and little interested in anything in life except the most practical things.

When fairly well developed you have a warm, friendly disposition, with an intense desire to please, and to be pleased. People with a well developed Mount of Venus are usually quite fond of music, dancing and other things which give pleasure.

If this Mount is too highly developed, so as to make the hand look lopsided, then you will have an extremely passionate nature, with little control over the emotions in so far as sex is concerned. This will be doubly true, if the Mount of the Moon is also highly developed, with a sloping Head Line and a strong Heart Line.

The Mount of the Moon

This is the Seat of imagination, intuition, and premonition. If the Mount is lacking, then all these things are absent. The person is very dull in the keener senses and has to work everything out in a cold, matter-of-fact manner.

If the Mount of the Moon is fairly well developed . . . appearing as a decided rise in the hand, near the wrist, then you have a healthy imagination, romance, intuition and the ability to follow first impressions correctly. If the Line of Intuition is plainly marked in the hand, with the first joints of the fingers supple and easily bent backwards, you have a person who "knows simply because he knows." He will probably not be able to give you a logical explanation as to his conclusions, but he is generally right. If the inner edge of the hand has a decided out-swing to it, with a well developed Mount of the Moon, then there is latent, or active creative ability of some sort; musical, literary or inventive.

None of the Mounts give such dangerous significance as does a highly developed Mount of the Moon. This bespeaks the person of diseased ideas, hallucinations, disordered mentality. If the Head Line is strong, then these indications are greatly softened. If the Head Line slopes right down into the Mount of the Moon . . . then neurosis, hypochondria, and undue nerv-ousness is indicated.

The Mount of Mars

As you will see by referring to the Map there are in reality two Mounts of Mars. When this sector of the hand is flat, then there is lack of "fight."

If the Mount of Mars is fairly well developed under the Mount of Mercury, you have self-possession, and generosity, but rather a boisterous nature . . . one who likes to brag about his ex-ploits. If the Mount is unduly developed, then there is violence, and extreme passion in temper and sex.

If Mars is well developed above Venus, then there is coolness in the face of danger, presence of mind in moments of emer-gency, and usually a taste for hazardous occupation or ad-venture.

If the Mount is developed to an extreme, then it shows a quarrelsome, unpleasant trait, which will sooner or later make itself known.

Mounts Leaning

As pointed out in the beginning of this chapter, you will seldom find the Mounts in the proper places. These have a habit of being to one side or the other of the finger where they truly belong, or will take a notion of leaning sharply to the right or left. You can easily tell which way the Mount may lean by tracing the lining of the cuticle to a point where it forms a rough sort of triangle, or apex.

Now for a few words about the proper interpretation of the leaning of the Mounts. We know what the meaning is of the Mount of Jupiter, if found directly under the Index finger. If this Mount of Jupiter leans forward toward Saturn, then you have a person who will possess all the attributes of one possessing a good Jupiter Mount, but, at the same time, will be of a serious nature.

If there happens to be a Mount of Saturn leaning toward the third finger, then that person would be more friendly and sociable than if the Saturn Mount were directly under the second finger.

So, from this, you can deduct in your own way, the meaning of the "leaning" Mounts, always keeping in mind this one thought . . . try to give positive interpretations at all times, rather than negative. Along this line, we again repeat what we have said before . . . make your hand analysis as encouraging to your subject as possible . . . not discouraging. Therefore, dwell upon his good qualities and magnify them, rather than stress his poor traits. Flattery, in the proper proportion is always advisable. In other words, decide when you go in for hand analysis, to be on the "construction crew rather than on the side of the wreckers."

Marks and Lines to Be Found on the Mounts

TO BE FOUND ON JUPITER

One Straight Line—General Success. High Ideals.
Two Straight Lines—Success rather uncertain. Idealistic.
Many Confused Lines—Too idealistic for material success.
A Definite Spot or Dot—Misfortune to the ideals. Loss of prestige.
A Cross—A happy marriage of an idealistic nature. (This is the

only place in the hand where a cross has a favorable meaning.)

A Star—Very high ideals . . . those which are usually achieved. This indication will be stronger if there is a good Head Line and thumb.

A Star and Cross—Usually where the idealistic marriage has also brought material success as well.

A Square—If unaffected by contrary lines in other parts of the hand, it means a protection of some sort. If affected, then a definite loss, sorrow, or other disturbance toward the idealism which tends to cynicism.

A Circle—(Very rare) Good fortune through a certain element of luck.

A Triangle—Definite disappointment in ideals . . . falsity of friends or loved ones.

A Grill—Not a good mark . . . usually means frustration of ideas and ideals. Requires much will power to overcome this mark.

TO BE FOUND ON SATURN

One Line—Financial security . . . if very deep and undisturbed then . . . success out of the ordinary, but through one's own efforts.

Confusion of Lines—Financial reverses and insecurity.

Diagonal Line—Possibility of Inheritance.

A Definite Dot or Spot—Tendency to nervous disorders . . . moodiness.

A Cross—Tendency to despondency . . . hermit-like, taciturnity.

A Star—If attached directly to one of the financial lines . . . one who will never want for the material things of life. Security in old age.

A Triangle—A tendency to be up and down in spirits.

A Grill—If there is a down-sweeping Head Line, too much imagination of the "destructive" sort . . . suspicion. If the Head Line is straight the influence is for a work which can be done alone . . . no particular love of public contact.

TO BE FOUND ON THE SUN

One Line—Good friends, but not many. Strong friendships. Success through friends . . . also through the arts. Love of people.

Two Lines—Unusual firmness in friendships.

Diagonal Line, Crossing Perpendicular Lines—Loss of friendships or disappointment in friends, marriage, engagement, love affairs, etc.

A Dot—Loss of social prestige or position.

A Cross—An emotion or friendship crossed out of the life.

Many Lines—Sometimes versatility in talents . . . again shallowness in friendships and affections. Easily influenced by "false" friends.

A Star—Distinction either through art, or public contacts.

A Star—With strong Sun Line . . . prominence. (In a man's hand, through his efforts, aided by friends.) (In a woman's hand prestige through husband.)

A Diamond—With strong Sun Line . . . Wealth or fame.

A Square—A disappointment or tragedy in friendships, love, marriage, etc. This will be more true if there is a break in the Fate Line.

A Circle—(Seldom seen) Possibility of much fame.

A Circle and Cross—Fame at one time, then lost. (Seldom seen)

Triangle—Breaking in friendships, or accomplishments by outside interference.

Grill—Not a good mark. Bragging attitude. Delusions of grandeur.

TO BE FOUND ON MERCURY

One Line—Keen mind. Executive ability.

Two Lines—Power of expression. Also executive talents.

Many Wavy Lines—Rather poor business judgment.

Many Short Distinct Lines—In a man's hand . . . quick thought. In a woman's hand . . . sharp tongue, gossip, sarcasm.

A Dot—Trouble in business.

Cross—Possible loss in business through faults of others. Treachery.

Circle—(Seldom seen) Fame in business or profession.

Triangle—Mental keenness, but too often scattered. Also can mean breaking of partnerships and losses through partners.

A Grill—Many ups and downs in a business way.

IF FOUND ON VENUS
(*Not to be confused with Travel Lines*)

Many Vertical Lines—Emotional . . . dependent upon love and affection.

Many Vertical Lines, Crossed by Short Horizontal Lines—Passion.

A Large Dot, or Spot—Unpleasant love affair, or engagement.

A Large Cross—Love affair, or marriage ending sadly.

A Cross—(Near Life Line) Death of close relative or friend in the past.

A Star—(Near Life Line) A happy event in love, friendship, marriage. Often the indication where a good marriage was consummated.

A Diamond—Many Friends. Happy Marriage.

A Square—A tragedy in affection. Generally unfairness in love from other party.

A Triangle—A triangle in love, engagement, or marriage. Sign of two affairs of the heart at one and the same time.

A Grill—Many disappointments in friendships and loves.

IF FOUND ON THE MOON

One Line—Strong imagination of a creative and constructive nature.

Many Distorted Lines—Not a good sign. Overactive imagination of a destructive nature.

A Dot or Spot—Disorders of some sort to the nervous system.

A Cross—Loss of friends through moodiness or changeable nature.

A Star—Can use intuition to good advantage. (Particularly if strong Line of Intuition is in Hand.)

A Circle—(Seldom seen) Excellent imagination in a creative way, particularly in the literary field.

A Diamond—Indicating where derogative imagination has been controlled and offering better mental security in later life.

A Triangle—Cunning and calculating disposition. Suspicious nature.

A Grill—Morbidness and a gloomy outlook on life. Fancied slights.

ON THE MOUNT OF MARS
(These lines can be found on either of the Mounts of Mars.)

One Line—Courage and aggressiveness.

Many Long Lines—Headstrong nature, with quick temper.

Spot or Dot—Danger of accidents through rashness.

Cross—Danger of bodily harm through temper.

Star—Will fight against all obstacles.

Diamond—Recognition through courage, usually military.

Triangle—Danger of bodily harm through secret enemies, or unexpected sources.

Grill—Danger of accident, or violent death.

Many Horizontal Lines—Possibility of enemies through thoughtlessness.

NOTE: All lines, on all mounts, are to be considered only if they are vertical, unless specifically designated otherwise.

8

ACTION OR
INFLUENCE LINES

Running across the Mount of Venus, starting from the thumb and heading toward the Life Line, the Action or Influence Lines are to be found.

At first, you may have difficulty in separating these from the Travel Lines and rightly so, because these are really co-related to each other; because travel is action, and in this definite influences are brought into the life. Then there will be a bit of trouble with the true Venusian Lines, explained previously. However, you will soon be able to master the puzzle, once you have the Key. Remember this—Travel Lines and the Venusian Lines are usually the stronger, while the Lines of Influence and Action are often faint, yet distinguishable. Furthermore, these Influence Lines head directly toward the Life Line and often break through it. The other sets of Lines seldom go through the Life Line, usually stopping at the Life Line. When one or more of these Influence or Action Lines actually crash through the Life Line, then something of importance has happened. The approximate time of the event can quite clearly be recognized by the decade system.

These Action or Influence Lines are what denote the difference from activity and "humdrum-ity." People with few of these lines, we have found, lead quite ordinary lives, with little to relieve the monotony of existence. True, the life may have gone along smoothly enough from a standpoint of health, finances and other events, but there has been a rub . . . it has been too monotonous . . . like the ticking of a clock . . . the same tomorrow as today . . . restricted and drab.

The location of these Lines are on the Mount of Venus, as this part of the hand is the Instinctive or Emotional sector. Therefore, the lines here indicate only hopes, wishes, desires . . . until these actually break through the Life Line. So, on your Mount of Venus, in your Action or Influence Lines, are all the problems, the work, the dreams, the hopes and the desires of a lifetime . . . and in many instances these remain incomplete . . . never realized.

Even in hands where few, if any, of these lines have broken through the Life Line, we have found when they were present, that the individual got a thrill out of living, planning, dreaming, "building air castles" even though these things may never become a reality.

However, it is when these Action or Influence Lines really cut clearly through the Life Line and then begin to twist, turn, dip and seemingly scoot to some other part of the hand, that you obtain evidence of really important events.

Now for the most important interpretations of the Action or Influence Lines. Unless otherwise specified, these will run in one direction, inclining to the Horizontal.

Lines across the hand, rising toward the Head Line: A period where there has been anxiety and worry about another person (such as illness, financial reverses, etc.).

Lines crossing the Life Line at its start: Illness in childhood. These are often more accurately read from the left hand.

Very deep Lines cutting across the Life Line: Illness of a serious nature . . . possible operations.

Short Lines dropping from Life Line, toward Mount of the Moon: Changes in business, occupation, location, under compulsion . . . not a good indication.

Short Lines dropping from the Life Line, on the thumb side: Changes in business, environment, location, etc. Usually for the better.

Long Line rising toward Saturn: Possibility of a new career, or where career has been changed . . . two occupations at the same time.

Line running to Mount of Sun: Very favorable change in location or business.

Line running to Mount of Mercury: Shifting from a mediocre career to something better . . . advancement mentally.

Line cutting across Fate Line: Loss of some sort, either through death or breaking of friendship. The stronger the line, the greater the loss.

Line cutting Head Line: Disappointment, or interference in education . . . also anxiety and worry over a long period of time.

Line cutting Heart Line: Disappointment in love affair or friendship.

Line running toward the so-called Marriage Lines: Troubles in domestic life. If cross on either Fate, or Heart Lines, near the third finger . . . quite often death of a husband or wife (in the past).

You must learn to interpret other Lines as you gain experience. Just bear this one fact in mind at all times: Every Influence or Action Line crossing the Life Line represents some important event in the past. Other marks and indications on the hand will soon give you the ability to read the whole story.

9

FINGERNAILS

The Fingernails tell quite a story in connection with the complete analysis of the hand, and should be considered if the whole picture is to be complete.

The nails not only give a good general idea of certain outstanding characteristics, but are also good criterions as to bodily or nervous health. Medical science recognizes this latter possibility and many physicians use the aspect of the nails in diagnosing certain diseases and note the patients progress by the change in the nails.

It is a well known fact that the length, color, shape and general condition of the nails will change from time to time, depending upon certain physical and nervous reactions in the body.

We have found the nails to be accurate in many ways, and we therefore urge you not to overlook these important adjuncts to the hand-proper in your analysis.

In studying the nails only, consider that portion which grows fast to the flesh, as the length, or shortness beyond the end of the finger is a matter of individual taste and has nothing to do with the true characteristics exhibited by the nail proper.

The only time the length of the nail is to be taken into account is when there is evidence of biting. You should almost know without explanation the type of person who will bite the nails

. . . nervous, irresponsible and not with the strongest character or will. As you study more and more hands, you will be surprised to find how many "nail-chewers" there are. Every time we run across such a person we try to instill the necessity of breaking off this very annoying and unpleasant habit which may lead to a wide variety of ailments and nervous disorders.

In Figure 9-1, we have given a diagram of the different types of nails most encountered. You will very often find different types of nails on the same hand. Without exception this will indicate a well rounded life . . . that is, a considerable amount of activity of various sorts. A person with this type of nail will not lead a humdrum existence, but rather one which has many interesting experiences. These nails are often found on the hand of persons who may have many ups and downs, but never drab, colorless lives.

There are two important facts to remember in reference to the nails. The longer and more narrow the nail, the more passive the temperament. The broader and shorter, the more active.

Now for our specific analysis of the nails. In order to ease the memorizing of the types of nails, we have given each one a name, in accordance with its number.

No. 1 "The Narrow Nail." This nail is usually found to predominate on the Psychic or Conic hand. More common to women than to men. This is truly the possessive nail. Its possessors are rarely fighters, but gain their point through arbitration and diplomacy. This type of nail usually indicates a rather sweet and even temper, unless other indications of the hand show extreme nervousness, then you will find the possessor inclined to self-pity. These nails on a hand with a good Life Line and Fate Line, indicate a rather smooth running life. It is also the artistic nail.

No. 2 "The Round Nail." This nail is nearly always on the Conic Hand. Occasionally on the Square Hand. This shows self-poise and evenness of disposition. It belongs to those whose existence is fairly well ordered through their own attitude toward life. These nails belong to the person who is particular in everything he does. He is fond of detail and can use patience in order

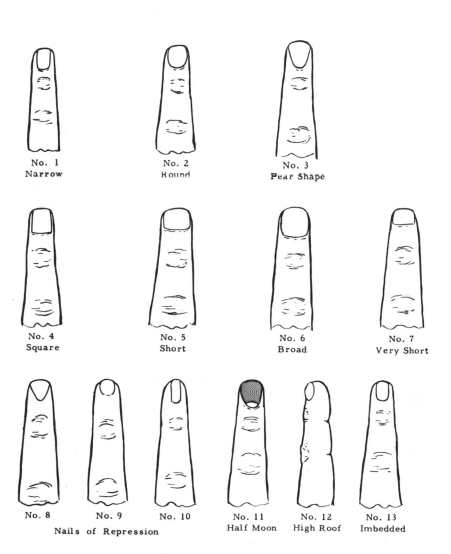

Fig. 9-1. Various types of fingernails.

to gain perfection. These nails nearly always show a good sense of humor and genuine friendliness. Inventive or creative ability of some sort are quite common to the round nail.

No. 3 "The Pear Shaped Nail." Wide at the end, pointed at the base. The impatient nail. The nail of the skeptic and critic. This nail is quite common on the Spatulate and Philosophic Hand. Seldom seen on the Conic or Psychic Hand. If so, it shows extreme irritability and fault-finding. If on the Square Hand it shows quick perception and thinking. Persons with this sort of a nail, are usually as critical of themselves and their own shortcomings as they are of others.

No. 4 "The Square Nail." Nearly always, this one is found on the Square Hand, particularly if the fingers are rather short and broad. Truly a man's nail, although it is sometimes seen on the hands of women, especially if her hand is broad at the base. This broad nail belongs to the businessman, or woman, the lawyer, the politician, newspaperman, etc., or any vocation where good judgment and certain aggressive faculties are needed.

No. 5 "The Short Nail." This type of nail is more broad than long. The person possessing it is impulsive in both action and speech, usually one who is ruled largely by passion, rather than by reason. If the short nail is on a good, strong hand, well lined, you will have an aggressive person . . . a dynamic personality in all things. If the hand is badly formed and badly lined, particularly from the emotional angle, then you will generally find unpleasant tendencies.

No. 6 "The Broad Nail." This nail is moderate in length but very wide and inclined to squareness at the base, where it joins the cuticle. It is to be found on the Square, Spatulate or Philosophic Hand, never on the other types. The Broad Nail is significant of good mentality, practicability and self-confidence, in a quiet sort of way. Breadth of mind and vision are also represented. The Broad Nailed person is usually a "good mixer," but chooses his friends. It is the nail of the businessman, scholar, scientist, physician, military man, or other profession which requires mental and physical abilities.

No. 7 "The Very Short Nail." This sort of nail is easily

recognized . . . it is far shorter than it is broad. It has some of the attributes of the pear-shaped nail . . . except that it is more violent in its criticism. Persons with this type of nail generally use so much energy "crabbing and complaining" that they seldom accomplish anything worthwhile. If this nail is found on short, thick fingers, with a stubborn thumb thrown in for good measure, you have a person who is opposed to everything . . . one who will argue until he is blue in the face that "black is white," providing that you have stated that "white is black."

Nos. 8, 9, 10 "Nails of Repression." We have found that nails which are entirely out of proportion to the fingers, as illustrated in the sketches, show repression of various kinds. Often these frustrations of emotions, desires, self-expression, etc. are engendered in childhood, through over-strictness on the part of the parents, brothers, sisters, or companions, which builds up within the individual as a decided inferiority complex. This inhibited condition will, to a greater or lesser degree, express itself throughout life. The form of expression often varies. You will find it in timidity, self-effacement, self-pity, depreciation of self and moral or physical cowardice on one hand. Then, in the reverse, you may find the person endeavoring to cover up his true self, which within him contains repression, with an outwardly show of quarrelsomeness, petty fault-finding, nagging, suspicion, cunning, domination by subterfuge, etc. In other words a "chicken heart within . . . a bluff without."

The suppression in these nails is always in greater ratio to the type of hand . . . the Psychic and Conic Hands will possess these nails more often than the Square, Philosophic or Spatulate. If seen on the latter three types, you will still have repression, but more ability to overcome it. Abnormal nails which are flat, have more of the Repression tendencies than those which have "High Roofs," (No. 12). Remember this . . . the flatter the nail . . . the more reserved the personality and the reverse.

No. 11 "Large Half Moons." Here is always a sure indication of the vital things of life . . . good health, good humor, activity, personality, friendliness, etc. You will find the half moons on all types of nails, but these predominate, and you can understand

why, upon the Round and Square type, also on the Broad. These
are seldom seen on the very short, broad nail, or on the extreme
"pear-shaped." They are quite frequent on the well formed long
slender nail. Rarely do you find them in the nails of repression.
The size of the half moons and the number of fingers on which
these appear is a good guide in gauging the temperament of the
person in accordance with the attributes just listed. Quite often
you will find a large well shaped half moon on the thumb, but
little or no evidence of this on the fingers. Then take into
consideration the shape, size and other conditions of the thumb
for your key to the interpretation.

No. 12 "High Roof Nail." This nail is directly opposite to the
flat nail, both in appearance and indication. The more narrow
the nail, the more "arch" to the "roof." The "High Roof" nail is
always indicative of an extroversive person, while the flat nail is
the opposite . . . the introversive. The person with the "High
Roofed" nail is friendly, cheerful, likes people, likes a good time
and is usually active. If this type of nail is connected with the
"Narrow Nail" you usually have a pleasant personality, one who
is a good mixer, etc. On the other hand, if you find this "High
Roofed" nail on the Round, Square or Broad Nail, it is indicative
of activity where personal contacts are concerned. But you will
have the same general friendliness as with the "Narrow Nail."

No. 13 "The Imbedded High Roofed Nail." As we stated
before, the imbedded flat nail indicates repression, therefore the
imbedded "High Roof Nail," would be the opposite . . . expression, but in a rather peculiar way. This expression often goes
into emotional passion, sensuality, love of earthly pleasure and
little real spirituality.

Finger nails are often used by physicians for diagnostic purposes. We have never gone in for this to any great extent as we
believe that affairs pertaining to the field of medicine have no
place in Hand Analysis.

However, we have noticed two or three things concerning
nails which you will find to be quite accurate.

You will nearly always find a hand which indicates nervousness, having ridged finger nails. These are also usually quite
brittle and break easily at the ends.

Persons who are subject to colds of the throat and chest will often have nails with a tendency to turn downward at the ends of the fingers when the nails grown long.

The cause of white flecks on nails is a controversial subject. Some authorities claim these are brought about by striking, or slightly bruising the nails; others say chemical deficiency in the body, usually calcium, is the cause. However, we have found these white flecks coming and going in the nails of nervous, high-strung persons. This fact seems to indicate that these "flecks" are barometers of emotions. When a period of tenseness, or nervousness comes then the flecks appear. When this passes, they disappear.

Nails, to be correct, should be naturally glossy and slightly pink. The nails should be hard, but not too thick or brittle. Such a type of nail indicates good health, good spirits, good taste and proper refinement in keeping with the type of nail. Lastly: The shape of the nail should correspond to the shape of the finger . . . i.e. the long, slender nail on the long slender finger . . . the broad, long nail on the broad long finger, etc. When there is abnormality you will find discrepancy somewhere in the general character and emotional makeup of the person. Study nails . . . you will find they speak volumes and help you to a greater understanding of the Story of the Hand.

10

ODDITIES IN THE HAND

In our many years of professional practice we have made many original discoveries of these peculiar oddities. To the best of our knowledge, many of these have never been mentioned or used in any other book on Palmistry. We have proved time and again, that these oddities are accurate. One of the most astounding discoveries we made concerns the family, and we offer as proof, the actual imprints of hands . . . we call these:

The Lines of the Family

For several years after we began the practice of Hand Analysis, we were puzzled by certain lines that were seen in every hand. Lines which lie on the outer edge of the palm and rise from the base of the palm, toward the little finger. See Fig. 10-1.

We experimented with one thing after another . . . but without success, and then, suddenly we found what we had been searching for . . . these were the Lines of the Family. When we say family, we do not mean the number of children there may be in the life of a man, or woman. (These, you recall are to be found on the wrists.) But rather the "home circle," the father, the mother, brothers and sisters, which make up the original family of the subject.

As in all other peculiar combination of lines in the hand, these require study for mastery.

To best look for the Family Lines, use a good light. Turn the outside of the hand upward. Look for the strong lines . . . the ones that are straight. It is wise for a beginner to ask this question and demand a fair answer: "Do not tell me the number in your family, but did you come from a small family?"

The reason for this question is this: You will often run into a hand which has a welter of lines on it. Frequently these are minor lines, which mean nothing, except in cases where relationship ties are close and will indicate close relatives, such as aunts, uncles, cousins, grandparents, etc. This has been proven true when these relatives have entered into and influenced the life of the subject.

By establishing the fact as to the relative size of the family, you will soon be able to pick out the major "Lines of the Family" and discard the ones that do not belong to the immediate family circle.

Now, for the establishment of the lines. You can use two methods. Using the lines of the father, mother and children, or, the children alone, which we have found to be most satisfactory.

As a general rule you will find the lines of the father and mother, cut rather deep and nearest to the Health Bracelet, which is always used as the Number One Line or the line which indicates the individual to whom you may be talking. However, this cannot be established as a fixed rule, as we have often found these lines high in the hand, or not even showing. When the parents' line lies close to the bracelet you will always find a close association between the parents and the child, an association which has not diminished with the years. The absence of the Lines of the father and mother indicate that both parents have been out of the individual's life for a long time, either through death or early separation. It is because of this confusion in regard to the father and mother lines that we recommend that a beginner try to select only the lines of the children.

The children in the family are shown by the longest and straightest lines. With care and practice you can count these exactly. You will sometimes see lines crossed or broken. These we have found to be representative of the children who are dead.

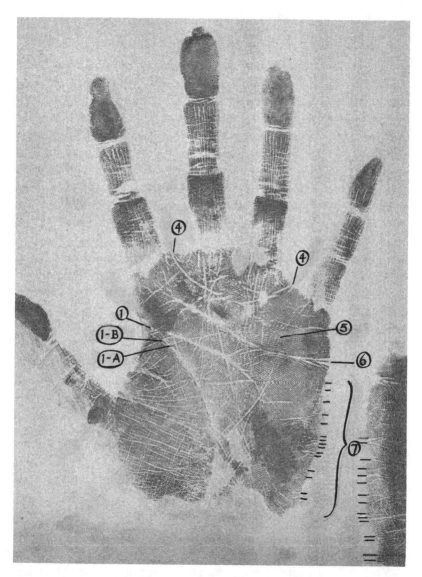

Fig. 10-1. Accurate lines of large family—also the mark of diabetes.

Very faint lines show those who died in infancy, many times these deaths occurred before the birth of the person whose hand you may be analyzing. It is always best to count up the entire group of lines because in doing so you will become more accurate and your subject will mention the deaths.

Quite often you will find an extra line or two in or near the actual Family Lines. Whereas in these there is a superfluity in so far as the true Family Lines are concerned, you will find that each of these extra lines, no matter how many there are, show the influence of another person . . . or relative such as a grandfather, grandmother, uncle, aunt, etc., living under the same roof, and actually being a member of the family. We refer you to Map of Oddities for an illustration of this complex group of lines. Lines A and B represent grandfather and grandmother.

We heartily recommend that you study these Family Lines intently. Master their interpretation as quickly as possible. Test them on your own hands and those of your friends. You will find them extremely fascinating and most interesting to those whose hands you may analyze. We have found the Lines of the Family to be the most astounding of any, and that includes Lines of Marriage, Children, etc. The reason for the interest in these lines is simple: Many individuals have had their hands analyzed by Palmists of every type, but they have told us again and again that we were the first and only ones who have brought out the Family Lines accurately. We therefore believe that we are the discoverers of this system and make this statement without fear of contradiction: This is the first time the location and explanation of these lines has ever been set down on paper.

We warn the student on one family group that will be difficult to be accurate on, and that is where there is only the one child. An only child is usually the darling of the grandparents, and as a result the family will appear to be larger, because the influence of the grandparents will always show if they have figured in the life of an only child.

You will also find that in the event of a step-parent this line will appear in ratio to the influence of that person.

During the year when we analyzed hands in one of Washington's largest department stores, we proved these lines beyond a shadow of a doubt. We were 99 and 9/10 per cent correct. The one tenth too often included the one child families.

Large Family and Diabetes

In this hand print (Fig. 10-1), we find several outstanding oddities. First the Lines of the Family (No. 7). In this instance there are 15 lines indicating 13 children and the parents. All lived and have attained maturity.

A little to the left (No. 5) is found the peculiar whirl, which in this case represents Diabetes in the immediate relationship.

Note the deep lines with a great many crossing the major Lines. The texture of the skin in the palm is rather coarse and this coupled with the many lines shows early health disturbances where fever played an important part. Note crossing on Life Line (No. 1-A).

The Large Square setting over the Life and Head Line, touching the Heart Line, is a decided indication of "Emotional Frustration" due mostly to the idealistic type of Heart Line.

We also find "The Girdle of Venus," (No. 4-4). In this hand it is more of the nervous type, rather than the artistic.

How to Determine Status of Husband
Another Startling Discovery:
(Herein we are again the first exponents.)

This is to be seen in the hands of all women where the marriage and emotional lines indicate marriage in the life of the individual. We have found a group of lines which will determine the classification of the vocation or occupation of the husband, either present or departed. In many instances we have found evidence of the vocation in the hand of a girl engaged to be married. Impossible, you say. No, indeed, not impossible, but a proven fact.

You will not be able, by this system to definitely say that the man in question is a "baker, butcher or candlestick maker" but you can classify him as belonging to one of the general divisions of vocation: Professional . . . Business . . . Executive . . . Salaried in a specific type of work . . . Trades and the allied branches of the Military.

This unusual analysis is made in the same general way as given in Chapter 5, where we discussed a man's Heart Line as an indicator or prognosticator of his occupation.

If, in a woman's hand, the Heart Line forks upward between the first and second fingers, you will find her husband in some definite profession . . . not always "on his own." He may be on a salary, but still be a professional as to his vocation, training, etc. We have found this to be very accurate in the hands of wives whose husbands have followed one particular type of work, such as government jobs, chemists, newspapermen, or civil engineers.

If the Heart Line runs perfectly straight across the Hand, then usually the man is in business for himself or holding a position in the business world where he has definite authority.

If the Heart Line runs straight across the hand with a slight upsweep toward the fingers, at the end, then the husband will be an executive type.

If the Heart Line turns down at the end toward the Head Line then you will find the husband in one of the trades.

If the Heart Line turns down at the end, toward the fingers and with another slight fork going toward the Head Line, then he is a salaried man . . . the larger the fork, usually the larger the salary.

Then there is another line, which requires considerable study in deciphering it correctly. We call this "The Line of Special Training." This line is quite similar to the Professional Line, but it has a more definite upsweep between the first and second finger. This is the line indicating that the husband is in some very specialized type of work. It is almost invariably seen in the hands of women who are the wives of Army, Navy and Marine officers. Strangely enough, when you contact one of these women, and definitely establish the fact that her husband is in the service, as an officer; you can tell his rank by a series of short, clear, upright lines, which run from the Heart Line to the base of the second finger. Each one of these lines, starting from the left side of the second Finger and counted toward the first finger, shows a rank. Of course, before you can be able to tell the rank, you must know the ranks of both Army and Navy. These are as follows: Army: 2nd Lieutenant, 1st Lieutenant, Captain, Major, Lt. Colonel, Colonel, General (Brigadier and Major). The Marine Corps has the same ranking as the Army.

In the Navy the rank goes as follows: Ensign, Junior Lieutenant, Senior Lieutenant, Lt. Commander, Commander, Captain, Rear Admiral, Vice Admiral and Admiral. You will seldom see these markings unless you are located where there are servicemen and their wives.

In connection with this analysis, the following incident happened while we were in the department store, analyzing hands.

A middle-aged woman came in for an analysis. When it came to the husband's vocation, the lines were correctly identified as being that of a serviceman. She was then told that her husband was a Colonel. She was too startled for a moment to speak. When she finally could, she said, "Several of my friends have told me you were able to tell from their hands, the rank of their husbands, and I thought they were exaggerating. You are absolutely correct, my husband is a Colonel."

These graduated lines have another meaning . . . showing that the husband is in some sort of work where he is advanced according to specific rules. This may apply to government service, police, fire department, railroading, etc. Again we warn you: These lines are "tricky," but can be read very accurately with practice and are indeed startling.

Let's go back to the Professional Line. Even though the husband may not be professional, in the full sense of the word, you can tell much about his progress in his own field of endeavor.

If the Heart Line forks upward, as explained in the Professional Line, but has a line which continues forward to the Mount of Jupiter, then that husband has gone into, or will go into something where he is more or less on his own. In any event, it means occupational and financial progress.

In learning to determine the meanings of these peculiar markings, remember this one important fact . . . The Line which goes to the Mount of Jupiter (beneath the first finger) always indicates independence from others in a financial way. Therefore, you may find the mark of the Executive, plus this line (which would indicate a man in business for himself) and at the same time, the chief executive of his affairs. Or you may find this same indication in connection with the mark of a Tradesman and discover that this man is a contractor for building, plumbing, heating, etc.

Here is one outstanding thing in connection with the husband's financial possibilities: When there is a straight line coming from the Heart Line which runs down between the first and second finger, and this line has a diamond shaped symbol on it, that woman will be fortunate enough to be married to a man who established himself financially either before their marriage, or shortly thereafter. This is especially true, if the Fate and Life Line are smooth and unbroken. In other words, the Diamond in this position indicates that the foundation for financial security was laid early in life.

You can also read the story of "occupation" by using this same method in the hands of women employed, and of course, quite clearly in the hands of men.

In the hands of older men and women, you will discover that if they have not followed through on the original type of work, you will notice tiny breaks in the "Lines of Occupation." By careful study you will be able to tell exactly how many changes the husband has made in his work.

We firmly believe that this is the first time that this group of lines has been used for this purpose and proven to be correct.

Malignant Diseases

We now offer you something extremely startling: That is the indications of Cancer, Diabetes, or Tuberculosis being in the immediate family or the close relationship. This does not apply to the individual, but entirely to the ancestry or present family.

These marks are to be found in that section between the Heart and Head Lines and in an area between the third and fourth fingers (See Family and Diabetic Map). Sometimes these markings will be discovered lower in the hand, occasionally near the Head Line or below it, or as far down as the Mount of the Moon, but these positions are rare.

The mark of Cancer is in the form of a slightly raised whorl in the flesh of the hand with a distinct pattern in the skin, like a finger print, and almost circle-like in formation.

The mark of Diabetes, or some other serious kidney ailment, is shown in a marking which resembles a horseshoe, rather than a circle.

The indication of Tuberculosis is more in the form of a triangle or some other peculiarity, or irregularity in the graining of the skin.

You will sometimes find two, three and possibly four such marks in the hand, sometimes all alike, sometimes different. We have had instances where three or four members of the family tree have passed on through one of these three mentioned ailments . . . then again, where two of the ailments have been in the relationship . . . or even all three.

The stronger and deeper these symbols, the closer to home has the illness struck; right into the immediate family—father, mother, brother, sister. The fainter the symbols, the further removed—grandparents, uncles, aunts, cousins, etc.

By accurate determination of these you can absolutely dumbfound your subject. When finding these indications, you must be careful to impress upon the person you are analyzing that these are indicators of past events and do not affect him in any way. You know there is a deadly fear on the part of many persons of hereditary diseases, although the medical profession has done much to explode this belief, so you can see why you must use extreme discretion and tact in handling these markings.

We have found these markings more pronounced in the hands of highly nervous individuals, who have either a conscious or subconscious fear of these malignant diseases if they have been present in the relationship . . . this is especially true of the cancer mark . . . *but we have never found one single instance where these markings were indicators of the disease in the body of the subject being analyzed.*

Letters in the Hand

Here is another interesting feature we have found . . . letters, usually initials of first or last names associated with the subject you are analyzing. Before discussing these, we warn you against the letter "M" which is to be seen in practically every hand. This letter is made by the Life, Head and Heart Lines. The letters you want to look for are the ones which are of real importance and these are to be found in other parts of the hand.

The most common place for these is in the general vicinity of the Life Line and toward the base of the palm. It is seldom that these letters will be found above the Heart Line, except those which may show up directly under the third finger. If they lie there, they are nearly always to be associated with the marriage partner, sweetheart or close friend.

The letters which lie very close to the Life Line are generally the initials of father, mother, brother, sister or the person himself. This is especially true if the individual was named for some ancestor.

These can also show the influence of some person in the life of an individual, but more often these are connected with the family.

In hands which showed large families, and where these families were close in their affections, we have many times picked out the initials and letters of the name of every member of that family.

When these initials are not associated with the immediate family and lie near the base of the palm, they will show influences yet to come. One of the most striking examples we ever encountered in this connection was seeing a large letter "R" in the hand of two gentlemen and a lady. These three persons were in one group when we analyzed their hands. The lady mentioned the fact that many years before another Palmist had pointed out this "R" and stated that this letter would definitely affect her life at some time in the future, as it was not in her family. Although the lady gave no credence to this prediction at the time it was given, nevertheless it came true, because both she and the two gentlemen were directly influenced and associated with a gentleman in the absolute top-flight circles of the Executive branch of the United States Government.

You will not always find these letters clear cut, far from it. Sometimes you will find them very faint, but still discernible. Sometimes you will find these at different angles and sometimes completely upside down. For instance, the letter "M" seen from one angle will be just that, but looking at it from another slant, it will be "W." In such a case you will quite often find both letters applying.

When no initials of any sort are to be found, you will generally discover a rather unemotional person. For example, where there is a large family and no letters show, there is little connection between the person and the immediate family. If one, or two letters show up, these will represent the one having the most influence in a life, or those who hold the greatest attraction.

Now a warning against deformities, scars, hereditary influences in shape, form and condition of the hand. These peculiarities must always be studied and definite evidence established as to their possible reason for being, before attempting to take them into the analysis.

You will occasionally find the "Club Thumb" mentioned in another chapter. The "Club Thumb" has been, in the past, generally considered the "Murderer's Thumb," but by no means can this be considered correct. You will often find the "Club Thumb" upon a hand which indicates every tendency but "murder." In such a case, you will discover upon inquiry that this is a "Hereditary" mark and will disprove the accepted theories.

Then there will be a small thumb, tiny fourth finger, one finger very crooked or a finger bent at the end. Sometimes these conditions are the result of accidents, deformities or hereditary. Therefore, again we say, ascertain the meaning of these peculiarities, before you make definite statements that may be negative and upsetting to your subject.

11

A TYPICAL
HAND ANALYSIS

General Observations

This hand (Fig. 11-1) is definitely classified as the "square palm, with medium short fingers." This gives the individual one outstanding characteristic . . . she is a born Executive . . . far better fitted by nature and inclination to give orders than to take them. We do not mean by this assertion to infer that there is unreasonableness. But we do mean that this lady is not suited to any unimportant, menial or subservient position. The squareness of the palm denotes practicability and clear reasoning.

The short fingers are found on the hands of those peculiarly suited to manage detail work. These are always significant of the planner, the doer, the one able to successfully direct the activities of others. It is also an indication of painstaking attention to any plan or idea. However, once this idea, or plan is mapped out, then the short fingered person must have someone else to do all the small detail.

The hand has very deep lines, indicative of two things. First: A severe fever of some sort in early life. Second and most important, strong emotions. However, the depth of the lines show that these emotions are ruled by sheer power of will.

The whole hand is extremely well balanced. Palm square,

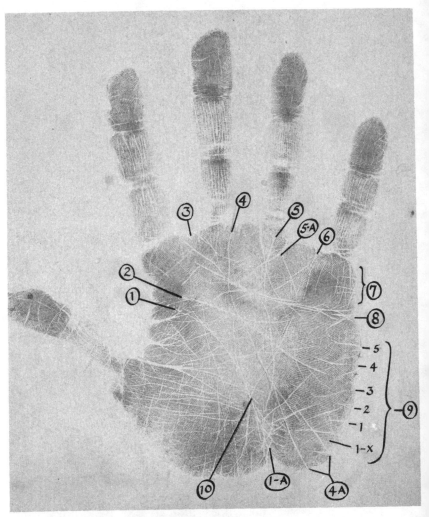

Fig. 11-1. A typical hand analysis.

fingers and thumb in proportion to the palm. Fingers wide and rounded at the ends . . . another indication of a well balanced nature. Sympathetic and friendly, but these attributes do not go so far as to distort the perspective on the true worth of things and people.

Fingers and Thumb

Notice the wide space between the fingers and the thumb as these join the palm. Nothing narrow in this individual's makeup. Generosity in everything is indicated here. Also a sincere desire and effort to try to see the other fellow's viewpoint.

The rounded tips of the fingers again show the executive ability and also indicate the capability for doing things with the hands, duties which require sureness and deftness of execution.

The index finger is straight. Here confidence is expressed in one's own ability. The second finger is unusually long which denotes definite ambition. The third is a trifle longer than the first, showing the ability to get along with people. The fourth finger is long . . . always indicative of power of expression . . . being able to convey to others thoughts and ideas in a clear concise manner. Another mark of the executive.

The fingers form a perfect arc as these join the palm. Here is shown balance of emotion, good control of temper and a tendency to take things in a rather philosophical sort of way.

The thumb is set medium high and is semi-rigid in structure. It has long phalanges which indicate high ideals and high ideas. This also shows one capable of going ahead on his own initiative. The rigidity of the thumb indicates a decided positiveness of mind, but there is sufficient flexibility to show adaptability. The thumb is rather narrow in the first phalange and has large joints . . . indicating tact and diplomacy.

The Lines

No. 1 *THE LIFE LINE* is a quite long, well formed and ends in a small diamond (No. 1-A). With this type of Life Line there should be good health, and a good life expectancy. The diamond has been proven to indicate freedom from financial worry in the latter years. The position of the Life Line at the end is important. This one ends right in the middle of the palm. Here is an indication that the subject will more than likely keep active throughout the entire span of life.

No. 2 *THE HEAD LINE* does not join the Life Line at the start, showing independence of thought and action. With this type of Head Line it is well for the individual to act largely on his own initiative, rather than take the advice of friends or relatives. Bisecting "Influence Lines" on the Head Line show changes of work during the lifetime.

No. 3 *THE FINANCIAL LINES*. There are several of these . . . a good indication, showing that the general financial situation will be well taken care of, from probably more than one source. When these Lines are as pronounced on a woman's hand as this imprint shows, that woman is usually well able to "paddle her own canoe" and prefers her financial independence and her job to that of a wife and homemaker.

No. 4 *THE FATE LINE* rises under its own finger, the second finger and runs directly through the hand, ending in a large fork (4-A). It is crossed three times, showing that Fate, or circumstances which could not be controlled, played an important part in the life, three times in the past. The outswing of the Fate Line, with the fork at the end, gives every indication that the subject will gain distinct recognition in some line of endeavor, during the latter part of life. This marking also indicates much activity and travel throughout the last half of life.

No. 5 *THE SUN LINE*. This line rises underneath the third finger and runs downward, toward the center of the palm, where it joins the Life Line. With the exception of a slight break of the Heart Line, this unusual line is continuous, indicating above average in the good things in life. Also, this shows, that the individual will take and keep her place in the Sun throughout the major years of life. The fact that there are two diamonds, connecting to the Sun Line (Fig. 5-A) further emphasizes security, in the beginning of life, which could come from inheritance, so some unearned source of income. The much larger diamond near the base of the palm indicates assurance of security in the very late years.

In connection with this Diamond near the base of the palm, it is interesting to note that it is almost always found in the hands of men and women who are likely to be eligible for pensions, social security and other forms of income protecting the subjects in their late years.

No. 6 *THE CAREER LINE* rises between the third and fourth fingers and runs down to the Life Line. It is crossed by both the Fate Line and Head Line and broken by the Heart Line. Here we find that some "affair of the heart" had much to do with the actual business achievement.

No. 7 *THE MARRIAGE and EMOTIONAL ATTACH-MENT LINES:* There are two of these. One crossed out, or broken through the center, indicating an early attachment which has been broken off. There is still one line intact which lies close to the base of the little finger, usually indicating a deep attachment late in life. But in view of the fact that the Career Line is so very strong, it is unlikely that the career would be interrupted by marriage.

No. 8 *THE HEART LINE* is broken at its start, and again under the third finger. Here is shown disappointment in friends, love affairs, etc., in the early part of life. However, the straightness of the line toward its end, indicates better luck in emotional attachments, friendships, etc. in the latter part of life.

No. 9 *THE LINES OF THE CHILDREN.* There are five of these, numbered from 1 to 5, indicating the five children in the family. The cross (1-X) shows that one of the parents is dead.

No. 10 *TRAVEL LINES* lie between the thumb and Life Line. There are many of these, indicating travel throughout the entire lifetime.

Actual History of Subject: This woman holds a very responsible position. In fact, she has reached the heights in her particular profession, as she has charge of a large number of nurses and directs their activities. Her life has been, and is, very active. She has worked against tremendous odds to achieve her present position. She has a warm, friendly disposition which makes her ideally suited for her work, but there is a degree of firmness in her makeup which makes her a good director. She can definitely be classified as a doer and not a dreamer. Hers is an outstanding example of the practical, level headed business woman's hand. One that shows that she is far more interested in her career than she would be to become dependent upon anyone else for her living. She is truly a career woman in every sense of the word.

12

HANDS IN ACTION

In the following pages we give you photographs and imprints of Hands in Action . . . Hands of individuals ideally suited for the type of work they pursue.

In the earlier part of the book, there are other Hands in Action . . . those well fitted in the scheme of life and vocation of their owners.

By studying all of these hands and the description given with each, you will recognize why, in every instance, there is a "round peg in a round hole."

The analysis of these hands show clearly the necessary traits so needed to enable these hands to perform their work and to do it well.

We believe you will gain much from these hands . . . you should be helped by studying them in gaining a clear insight into the fact that Hands *can* and should be considered as being quite revealing, as to the talent, liking or possibility for various vocational pursuits.

As we said in another chapter, unfortunately there are too many misfits in the scheme of life . . . those who have drifted into something for which they are not fitted by nature, makeup or desire. Therefore, if you can help someone to find his or her place, you will truly perform a worthwhile and splendid service.

A Muscular Hand for Steadiness

In this hand (Fig. 12-1), we ask you to give particular attention to the thumb. Here is an instance where the type of work has to a large degree changed the structure of the hand. You can almost see that thumb fit over the trigger of a pistol.

The hand is distinctly muscular, with extremely straight fingers. The first finger is slightly longer than the third finger. Very likely another development brought on by the constant handling of a pistol, for it has taken much practice, patience and perseverance to become a crack pistol shot (Fig. 12-2).

Here the Fate Line and Heart Line join. There are tiny branches running toward the base of the second finger. Here is a good example of a grouping of lines which we have proven to indicate the financial possibilities.

These fine branches represent the type of vocation where there is definite possibility of advancement and steps of progress.

Hands Created for Precision

Here is the true exponent of a hand capable of doing research work (Fig. 12-3). The short, blunt fingers indicate an interest in facts, not theories. The thumb is set low on the hand and this, coupled with its flexibility, shows an inherent friendliness. The sloping Head Line emphasizes this fact, as we have found that this type of Head Line is found on the hands of those who are "incurably sentimental." They are the kind of people who will remember little things and when this line is backed up by a strong, deep Heart Line, the individual will not likely forget birthdates, anniversaries, etc.

Take a good look at those nails (Fig. 12-4). They are almost perfect in their roundness. We have found a decided connection between the Round Nails and the length of the Life Line. Invariably there is always a long, strong Life Line in that hand possessing such nails. In other words, a well rounded nail indicates "a well rounded out life."

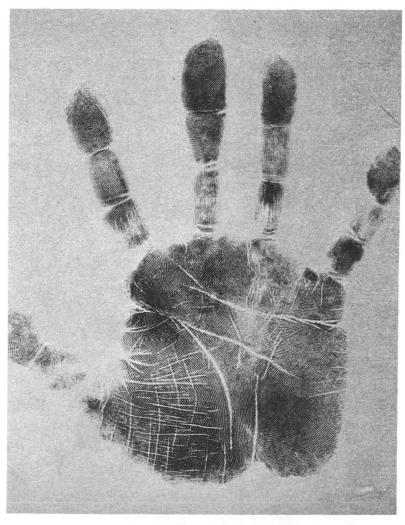

Fig. 12-1. A muscular hand.

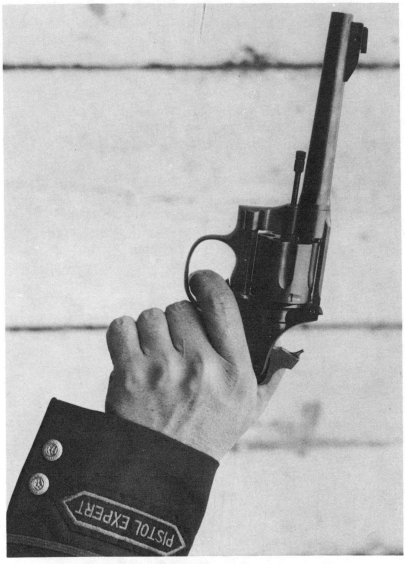

Fig. 12-2.

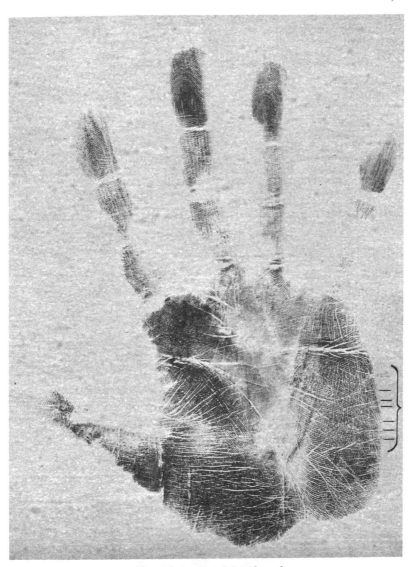

Fig. 12-3. Precision hand.

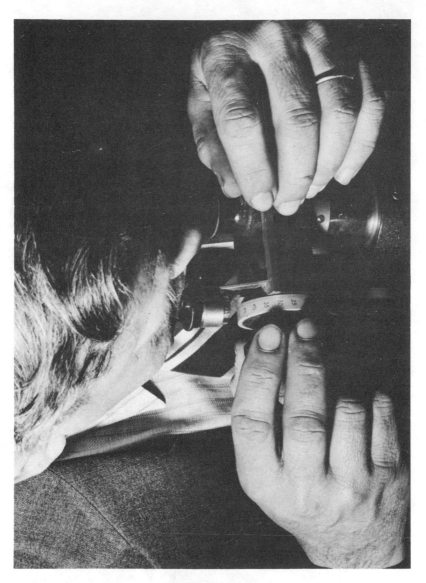

Fig. 12-4.

The seven lines marked on the outer side of the hand show the exact number in the family.

Incidentally the machine seen in this picture is used in the Bureau of Standards at Washington, D.C. and is a measuring machine capable of adjustment to an almost incredible fineness.

A Flexible Hand for Speed

The young lady whose hand is pictured here (Fig. 12-5) is ideally suited for her chosen career, that of a secretary.

Her long, round tipped fingers, with the first and third fingers in perfect balance as to length, show her thoroughness and accuracy.

It is not surprising that she won speed tests, when you examine the straight Head Line (Fig. 12-6). She was just naturally determined to succeed. Her Heart Line indicates deep emotions, but these are kept in control by the perfect joining of the Head and Life Line, which always indicates that the individual "rules by reason, rather than by emotions."

This is also the hand that would do well in the teaching profession, as the flexibility of the thumb shows patience and the attributes it takes to be a good teacher.

We spent several seasons in a mid-western town where there was a large teacher's college. It was interesting to find that when the summer school students (practically all teachers) came in for analysis, their hands were startlingly similar in design and outline. Here was one profession in which certain requirements given by nature were necessary for success. This was especially true of the thumbs. In the majority of subjects the thumbs were "narrow-waisted" and flexible; these were the natural born teachers, and most of them had many years of teaching experience to their credit. Wherever we found one with a rigid thumb, we found one who was dissatisfied with the profession; in almost each case they agreed that it tried their patience and made them nervous.

Fig. 12-5.

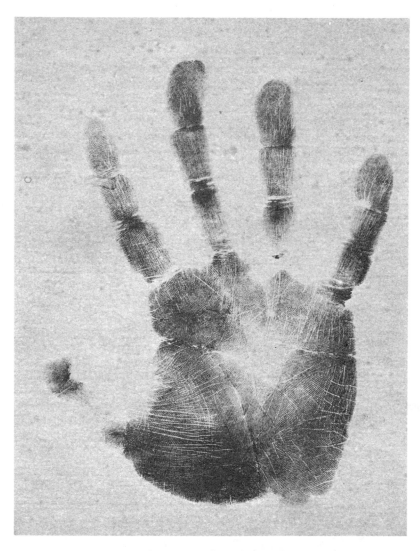

Fig. 12-6. Flexible hand.

A Typical Surgeon's Hand

In searching about for hands that were typical of the profession or vocation they were following, we chose the hand of a young surgeon, as illustrated by Fig. 12-7.

You should study this hand carefully. Noting particularly the unusually long fingers with almost psychic tips, indicating a sensitiveness to the ailments of his patients that should stand him in good stead.

His hands are soft, flexible with fine textured skin.

The thumb is flexible and long in all phalanges, showing adaptability, and being low set on the hand, shows friendliness.

The financial lines are typical of those found in the hands of a professional man (Fig. 12-8). These indicate that he will build his finances by slow degrees.

His hand print is very dark, due to the fact that the doctor was more nervous about having this simple "operation" performed than he would have been to perform one himself. Hence the moisture, or "sweating" of his hands, made it impossible to get a really good print.

And this brings out a point in our work. We have found that individuals, especially men, will almost "shake in their boots" when they are to have their hands analyzed. We have asked them about this fear, and in most instances the answer has always been the same: "I was afraid you would tell me something terrible was going to happen to my family or myself."

So, while men seem to be the scoffers, we have found they assume this attitude to hide their fears.

Women as a rule have an insatiable curiosity about themselves and every member of their families. And they usually want to know everything from A to Z.

In this photograph is a type of nail seen frequently. A nail that is broad at the end, but narrow at its beginning. Here is a man ideally suited for his particular type of work.

We have proven that this type of nail indicates moderation in all things, with a tendency toward suppression of the emotional

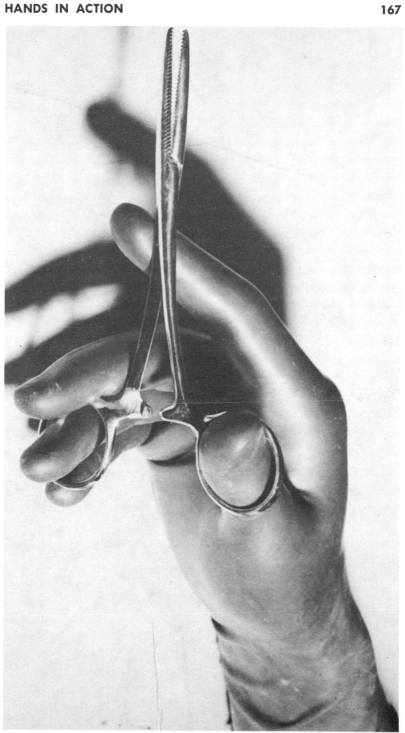

Fig. 12-7.

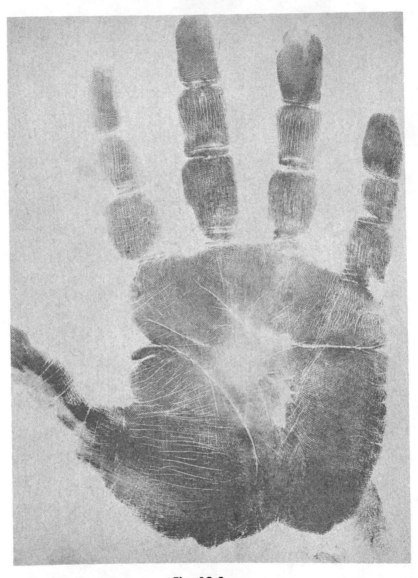

Fig. 12-8.

side of the nature, but with an ability for self-expression that is good.

Study this imprint. In it you will find the Fate Line extending throughout the entire length of the hand and you will notice the Career Line (No. 3) extends down to the Fate Line. Fate or Chance did not play an important part in choice of career. Rather it was definitely decided upon early in life.

However, the Financial Lines, lying beneath the second finger are distorted. This man will not make a lot of money at his profession, but with the Heart Line running across the hand, he will be doing the kind of work which best suits the dictates of his spiritual nature.

13

TEST YOUR KNOWLEDGE OF THE HAND

Is The Hand:
1. Flexible and soft to the touch?
2. Firm and hard, with little give?
3. Hard with no flexibility?
4. Unresponsive in a handshake, inert?
5. Fleshy, inclined to pudginess?
6. Cold?
7. Warmer than normal?
8. Long and slender?
9. Unusually short?
10. Medium in structure (neither long nor short)?
11. Too white in color?
12. White, where color does not change with heat or cold?
13. Unusually red, bordering on purplish?
14. Naturally brown (not tanned)?

You are correct if your answers were:
1. Friendliness, Mentally alert, Reasonable, Adaptable, Generous.
2. Self-reliance, Positive, Aggressive. Wants comfort but needs to be physically active.

171

3. Stubbornness bordering on obstinacy. If fingers are long, slender and pointed there is lack of alertness, mentally dull.
4. Lack of self-confidence. Inclined to self-centeredness.
5. Wants physical comfort. Seeks pleasure. Good disposition. Tolerant. Inclined to mental indolence.
6. Seemingly unemotional and reserved. Inwardly warmhearted, generous and impulsive.
7. Lots of personal magnetism. Quick temper. Usually vivacious.
8. Artistic appreciation (not necessarily an artist). Love of finer things. Excessively long indicates lack of tolerance, and impatience.
9. Ability to work with hands. Usually logical. Too short indicates argumentativeness bordering on quarrelsomeness.
10. A versatile person. Can act in emergencies. Good reasoning, an arbitrator.
11. Lack of energy, due to physical condition. Emotional but mostly artificial and on the surface.
12. Egotism. Intolerance. Hard to convince. Lack of perception.
13. More red than flesh colored . . . extreme optimism, need physical activity. Usually impatient. Inclined to be purplish . . . some health disturbance . . . bringing about inertia.
14. Keen Minded. Ambitious, desire for progress. Too lean (skinny). Domineering and abrupt in speech. If yellowish, highly nervous. Easily impressed. Artistic to an extreme, but lack of stick-to-itiveness, needs encouragement.

SELF QUIZ ON THE PALM

Is the Structure of Palm:
1. Square and firm to the touch?
2. Moist (sometimes clammy)?

3. Unusually dry, almost parched?
4. Smooth to the touch?
5. Rough and harsh to the touch?
6. Pale, lacking in color?
7. Splotched pink and white in color?
8. Are the lines scarce?
9. Moderate number of lines?
10. Very many lines, clearly defined?
11. Are lines crisscrossed and blurred in great confusion?

When hand is held open, in relaxed position, is there a wide space between:

12. The thumb and first finger?
13. The first and middle finger?
14. The middle and third finger?
15. The third and little finger?

These answers are correct:

1. Excellent reasoning power. Versatility. Courageous, physically and mentally. Good sense of Loyalty.
2. Lack of physical and mental drive. Sensuality. Deceitful.
3. Selfishness. Desire for personal gain. Nervousness and often victim of imaginary ailments.
4. Good, quick judgment. Intuitive. Impressionable. Love of comfort.
5. Strong character, but abrupt and harsh. Pride, physically active. Good logic and judgment.
6. Emotionally unstable. Introspective and pessimistic. Low vitality. Moody.
7. Irritability. Quick tempered. Outspoken. Holds grudges.
8. Strong mentality. Excellent poise. Courageous. Friendly, good natured. Not necessarily a mental type.
9. Energetic and versatile. Good vitality. Keen minded. Patience and perseverance.
10. Deep emotions not always controlled. Need to develop concentration. Excellent mental capacity. Apt to scatter forces. Inner nervousness.

11. Instability. High strung. Impatient. Lack of judgment. Not overly considerate of others.

When Hand is open and relaxed:
12. Generosity. Sympathetic, Understanding, Usually broad-minded.
13. Ambitious. Self-reliant. Independent in thought and action.
14. Unconventional ideas. Dislike of restraint.
15. Independence, can become arrogance. Initiative. Self-willed. Great determination.

THE THUMB

Is The Thumb:
1. Well-proportioned as to length and size?
2. Too short in either phalange (joint)?
3. Is the tip pointed?
4. Round-tipped?
5. Square-like tip?
6. Club-shaped?
7. Thick from front to back?
8. Exceptionally thin or flattish?
9. Knotted (with bulging knuckle or knuckles)?
10. Rigid-jointed making thumb stiff and unyielding?
11. Flexible and supple?

Remember these answers:
1. Intellectual. Determined. Good reasoning. Emotional control.
2. Lack of ambition. Governed by passions. Hot tempered.
3. Intuition (often uncontrolled). Superstitious. Sensitive.
4. Good judgement. Versatility. Even tempered.
5. Stubbornness. Lack of tact. Argumentative. Loyalty.
6. Cruelty. Obstinacy. Thin or flat, pessimistic, lack of will. Melancholy.
7. Love of material things. Enjoys good food, often over-indulges.

8. Keen minded. Quick witted. Lacking physical energy.
9. Too cautious. Ambitious but inclined to move too slowly.
10. Opinionated. Fixed ideas. Tactless. Uncompromising.
11. Tact and diplomacy. Graciousness. Determination. Good companion. Flexible in thought and action. A most desirable type of Thumb.

SEGMENTS OR PHALANGES (JOINTS)

1. Is the first (nail) phalange longer than the second?
2. Short, rather thick and stiff?
3. Short, thin from front to back, seemingly flattish?
4. Is it broad and well proportioned?
5. Is it almost equal in length with the second (lower) phalange?
6. Is the second (lower) phalange overly long?
7. Is it very short?
8. Is it "narrow waisted" with hollow curves into each side?
9. Is the thumb low set on palm and curves backward when extended?
10. Does it set close to palm when hand is relaxed?
11. Does the thumb rest inside when hand is relaxed?
12. Does it rest outside the fingers, almost fist-like when relaxed?

These answers are correct:
1. Determination. Strong willed. Will argue to gain his point.
2. Underlying coarseness. Quick temper. Gross instincts.
3. Lack of ambition. Mentally slow and underdeveloped. Indifference.
4. Great initiative. Personal pride. Executive ability. Firmness.
5. Stubbornness. Inertia. Gain through passive resistance.

6. Good judgement. Logical, fairness. Optimism. Perception.
7. Touchy. Petty. Unreasonable. Overly emotional.
8. Good intuition. Tactful. Refined. Balance between reason and emotions. Pride in achievement.
9. Friendliness. Generosity, love of people. Sometimes a graceful liar. Too good a fellow. Non-conformist.
10. Stingy. Self-centered. Secretive. Lack of friendliness.
11. Lack of physical stamina. Mental deficienies. Lack of courage. Leaners. Undecided.
12. Courageous. Great concentration. Physically active. Ability to make decisions. Can do any work requiring energy and stamina. Often argumentative. Pugnacious.

THE FINGERS ARE IMPORTANT

Are The Fingers:
1. Are the fingers long? Tapering? Some blunt? Others pointed?
2. Are the fingers short?
3. Is first (index) finger longer than third, or do they balance?
4. Is second finger much longer than others?
5. Is little finger very short, standing away from others?
6. Does little finger extend to first phalange of third finger?
7. Are fingers knotty with large prominent knuckles?
8. Smooth?
9. Rigid and stiff (not from arthritis)?
10. Supple, easily flexed?
11. Are any phalanges out of proportion, exceptionally long or short?

This analysis will help you:
1. Long tapering fingers indicate artistic ability. Some blunt, others pointed gives indication of versatility.
2. Quick tempered. Fast decisions. Irritated with detail. Good in managerial jobs. Obstinate.

3. Detailist. Evenly balanced, capable in routine work. Even temper. Level-headed.
4. Domineering. Outspoken. Good vitality. Energetic.
5. Independent. Petty. Quarrelsome without reason.
6. Imagination. Ability to speak fluently. Creative.
7. Philosophical. Orderly thinking. Good judgement. Reasoner.
8. Impulsive action. Artistic appreciation. Lacking in determination.
9. Slow thinkers. Fixed ideas. Not co-operative.
10. Quickness in thought and action. Versatile. Adjustable.
11. Long First Phalange: Idealist, intuition, poise.
Long Second Phalange: Ambition, originality, initiative.
Third Phalange: Self-esteem, prideful. Good organizer.

Tips of Fingers:
1. Are these Pointed?
2. Rounded?
3. Square?
4. Blunt sort of Club-shaped?
5. Mixed. Some round, some pointed or square?

Here are tips for you:
1. Psychic Power (often too sensitive). Lack of endurance. Irritable. Frivolous. Love of art and beauty.
2. Easy going. Optimistic. Even tempered. Versatile.
3. Out-spoken. Independent. Strong emotions. Inclined to grossness. Must get things done, quickly.
4. Energy, if lower phalange is long. Thick, Club-shaped— mechanical ability. Flaring temper. Unyielding. If flat, desire for recognition. Talent for stage and public work.
5. Quick reactions. Adjustability. Responsible. Accomplished in several types of endeavor.

Do the Fingers:
1. Bend backward when hand is stretched out and open?
2. Curve closely over the palm, when relaxed?

Answers:
1. Good common sense. Adaptability. Desire to co-operate. Quick thinkers. Good reasoners.
2. Greed. Stinginess. Self-centered, close-mouthed, pessimistic. Eccentric.

Take a Look at the Fingernails:
1. Are these long?
2. Short and curved?
3. Short and flat?
4. Pale almost white?
5. Bluish?
6. Ridged with rough edges (tendency to break easily)?
7. Curved over at end, talonlike?
8. Absence of halfmoons?
9. Prominent halfmoons?

"Nail" these answers in your mind:
1. Good disposition. Reserved. Sometimes timid.
2. A skeptical person. Argumentative. Good vitality. Energetic. Square at base . . . Very critical. Egotistical. Opinionated.
3. Lack of vitality. Inwardly emotional. Petty and critical.
4. A colorless person. Timidity. Lack of stamina.
5. Circulatory difficulty. Irritability. Often impaired health.
6. Nervousness. Health disturbance. Suppressed emotions. Restlessness. Uncontrolled temper.
7. If overly rounded, extreme passions. Health disturbances. Sensitive throat and lungs.
8. Low resistance. If nails are flat . . . tendency toward mental upsets. Lack of strength.
9. Good vitality. Generous. Energetic. Physically strong. Needs activity in type of work. Quick recovery in every way.

THE LIFE LINE

Is The Life-Line:
1. Deep . . . Unbroken. Clearly defined?
2. Broken in one or more places?
3. Chained (link-like). Badly formed?
4. Slightly curved (lying close to base of thumb)?
5. Very curved toward center of palm?
6. Long, ending in center of palm?
7. Quite short?
8. Double (parallel line most of length)?
9. Several short parallel lines?
10. Crossed and intersected by short lines?
11. Pale and colorless?
12. Redder than normal?

Analyze this line carefully: (*Most important*)
1. Good resistance. Health, strength and vitality. Energetic.
2. Health disturbance. Abrupt changes.
3. Nervousness. Irritability affecting health. Great upsets.
4. Emotional control. Prefers unchanged life. Fixed pathway.
5. Active life. Desire for public acclaim. Recognition.
6. Long active life. If forked near wrist . . . Protected old age.
7. Uninteresting life. Lack of determination. Not energetic. Not a vital life.
8. Health and vitality unusual. Good mental capacity. Ambition.
9. Much interference in life, from family and opposite sex.
10. Unplanned changes. Many worries. Unusual responsibilities.
11. Lack of resistance. Low vitality. Health impairment.
12. Quick, violent temper. Coarseness and brutality.

Does The Life Line Begin:
1. Beneath first finger, connected to Head Line?
2. Is there a space between the two lines?

3. Does it begin low, close to base of thumb?
4. Does it begin above Head Line, near the base of first finger?

Answers:
1. Normal mental and physical development. If the two lines continue toward the center of palm, sensitiveness and lack of confidence.
2. Indecisiveness. Hypochondriac. Erraticness. Stubborn. Health affected by emotional outbursts.
3. Tremendous physical energy. Self-confident. Success through determination and effort. Independent.
4. Recognition and success early in life . . . Will power. Ambition. Foresight.

Does The Life Line End:
1. Near the center of palm, close to base of thumb?
2. At the wrist almost touching the ("wrist-bracelet") lines?

Answers:
1. Lack of vitality. A drab life. Not ambitious because of health.
2. Usually a long life. Healthy old age.

Does it Branch:
1. At the beginning, with many fine lines?
2. Do the branches turn upward toward base of first finger?
3. Upward toward the Head Line?
4. Downward toward the center of the palm?
5. Are there pronounced branches toward the wrist?

Answers to questions on branches:
1. Wealth, success and honor gained through personal endeavor and mental activity (not physical prowess).

2. Financial independence achieved through perseverance. Great ambition. Energy and vitality in abundance.
3. Material success and recognition. Power and wealth. Happiness comes through distinction.
4. Frequent disappointments. Much effort to gain success.
5. Continued activity in old age. Mentally and physically active in latter years. Desire for friends and public acclaim. Improved security in late years.

THE HEAD LINE

Is The Head Line:
1. Clear cut, well-defined and unbroken?
2. Broken in more than one place?
3. Straight (sometimes across the palm)?
4. Does it have chain-like links?
5. Decidedly curved?
6. Long, curving downward toward outer edge of palm?
7. Is it short?
8. Double in one or more places?
9. Pale (almost colorless)?
10. Red (inclined to spotty)?
11. Intersected and broken by short lines?

Study these answers carefully:
1. Strong controlled emotions. Good co-ordination between mind and body. Analytical ability. Righteous judgment.
2. Irritability. Vacillating. Temperamental. Lack of concentration. Nervous. (Criminal Instincts.)
3. Very strong will. Good business ability. Independence of thought. Self-willed. Obstinate. Sense of fairness. Head rules heart.
4. Imagination. Creative. Lack of confidence. Easily imposed upon.
5. Lack of initiative. Low physical vitality. Petty and nervous.

6. Creativeness in many fields of endeavor. Desire of knowledge. Secretiveness.
7. Practicalness. Positiveness. Business ability. Outspokenness.
8. Ability in more than one line of endeavor. Changeable. Restless. Apt to scatter energy. A nagging disposition. Lack of vision.
9. A pale Head Line: Indecisive. Gullible. Mentally sluggish. Often moody and pessimistic.
10. Strong willed. Dynamic in action. Determined. Quick tempered. Explosive outbursts. Interested in almost all physical activities.
11. Small intersecting lines indicate: Easily swayed. Lack of concentration. Deep intersecting lines show: Nervous and emotional upsets. Ability to overcome disability, if Head Line remains unbroken.

Does The Head Line Begin:
1. Inside the Life Line (nearer the thumb)?
2. Is it attached to the Life Line (between thumb and first finger)?
3. Above Life Line (near first finger)?
4. Is it connected with Heart Line and Life Line (an oddity)?
5. Does it begin away from Life Line toward middle of Palm?

Consider these correct answers carefully:
1. Inclined to worry. Nervous temperament. Easily upset.
2. Independence of thought and action. Courageous. Self-discipline.
3. Ambition. Foresight. Self-important. Hasty judgement. Contradictory.
4. Strong family influences (to point of domination). Lacking in ambition and will power. Heart rules head.
5. Affected by early environment. Lack of confidence. Swayed by others. Emotional instability. (If head line is chained . . . Hysterical.)

Does The Head Line End:
1. In the center of the palm?
2. Well across the palm, curving downward toward the wrist?
3. Curve upward toward the little finger?
4. Does it end abruptly in a straight line?
5. With several forks or branches?

Answers and analysis:
1. A frivolous nature. Abruptness. Dominating. No desire for mental progress. Changeability. Little depth of character.
2. Creativeness in art or literature. Originality in ideas. Flexibility in thinking. Good sense of rhythm. Appreciation of color and harmony. Imagination (yet practical).
3. Desire for Material Gain. Psychic. Interested in occult. Emotions rules head. Lacking in self-control in many ways.
4. Excellent balance between head and heart. Determination to gain. Desire for recognition. Practical in ideas and action. Outspoken.
5. If there are several forks, beyond center of hand . . . desire for greater learning. Usually advancing career through study. In woman's hand, independence after marriage through extending career or taking up new career. An excellent indication for achievement through own efforts. A desirable asset for advancement in life.

Does It Lie:
1. Low, near the Life Line?
2. High, near the Heart Line?
3. Does it have many branches running from it?

Answers:
1. A cheerful disposition. Generosity.
2. The head will always rule the heart.

3. Fickleness. Desire for change. Lack of concentration. Nervousness.

THE FATE LINE

Is the Fate Line:
1. Clear-cut, well defined and long?
2. Are there breaks in one or more places?
3. Made up of several small lines?
4. Double?
5. Intersected by short lines?
6. Accompanied by several short parallel lines?

Answers:
1. Positive personality. Success through own effort.
2. Ups and downs in fortune. Uncertain career. Complete change in life.
3. An undecided person. Lack of progress. Disappointments.
4. An exciting, eventful life. More than one career. Strongly influenced by unexpected contacts. Quick decisions, pay-off.
5. Outside interference in career. Domination throughout life.
6. Divided interests. Never free from outside influences and interference.

Does It Begin:
1. At or near "bracelet" at the wrist?
2. At the Life Line?
3. Near the middle of the palm?
4. On the outer edge (opposite thumb)?

Answers:
1. Success in spite of many obstacles.
2. Recognition, wealth through one's own efforts.
3. Seemingly unlucky early life. Unhappiness through others. Late success and security.
4. Good, practical imagination. Optimism. Creative ability.

Is The Heart Line:
1. Clear cut. Well defined?
2. Broken in one or more places?
3. Are there tiny dots on it?
4. Is it long, reaching almost across the hand?
5. Short?
6. Thin, almost obscure in places?
7. Double?
8. Pale and colorless?
9. Red, with purplish tinge?
10. Are there small lines intersecting the Heart Line?

Answers:
1. Deep affections. Self-sacrificing nature. Big-hearted. Lasting attachments.
2. Fickleness. Disappointments in love. Disillusionment. Changeable affections.
3. Some health disturbance. Moodiness. Broken romances. Lack of vitality.
4. Lasting love and devotion. Strong sense of loyalty.
5. Selfishness. Sensuality. Love of self. Little warmth.
6. Egotism, exaggerated self-importance.
7. Humanitarian. Great love and affection. Demonstrative. Love of people. Friendly. Outgoing. Self-sacrificing.
8. Inability to express affection. Indifference. Self-centered.
9. Deep passions. Quick love affairs. Jealousy. Unreasonableness.
10. Unlucky in love. Many love affairs. Light affections.

Does It Begin:
1. On the Mount beneath the first finger?
2. Between the first and middle finger?
3. On the Mount beneath the middle finger?
4. Does it connect with Head and Life Line above the thumb?

Memorize these answers:
1. Strong love. Affectionate. Idealistic type of love.
2. Deep devotion. Lasting love and attachments. Love of people.
3. Introvert. Petty jealousy. Love of material things.
4. Devoted to family and friends. Good emotional balance. Generous. Need of approbation.

Does It End:
1. Beneath the third or ring finger?
2. On line with the little finger?
3. Well over the outer edge of hand?

Answers:
1. Conceit. Self-pride. Vanity.
2. Love because of material gain (calculated love).
3. Generous love. Very romantic. Affectionate and demonstrative.

Does It Lie:
1. Low, near the Head Line?
2. High in the hand (toward base of fingers)?

Answers:
1. Heart ruled by head. Insincerity in love and affection.
2. Highly emotional. More than one love affair. Impulsiveness.

Are There:
1. Branches running from it (sometimes intersecting it)?

Answer:
1. Toward the Head Line indicates conflicting emotions. To the base of the first (index) finger: Deep affections. Between first and second finger: Success and happiness. Love of public contact. At the end of Heart line: Humanitarianism. Deep sympathy. Loyalty.

14

ANALYSIS OF
FOUR ACTUAL HANDS

Analysis of Fig. 14-1

This is a most unusual hand imprint. It reveals so many important facts in the life of the individual.

This is the hand of a woman with tremendous determination as indicated by the extended Head Line (No. 1). When this line is joined to the Life Line at its originating point, between the thumb and first finger, that person definitely rules their life with reason. However, the Head Line, under the second finger, curves downward toward the outer edge of the hand. It continues to branch, showing continual mental growth and desire for knowledge, resulting in self-improvement. (This woman, born in a foreign country, got her high school diploma through night school after forty.)

The Head Line has three main branches. This woman's interests and abilities are widely diversified:

First she was a wife and mother.

Then she became a creative writer. From the imaginative, creative line (No. 2) a strong line is extended, with many small branches.

She is now teaching Creative Writing, also acting as a literary

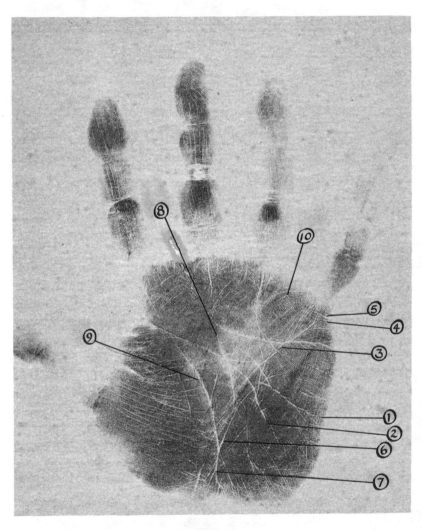

Fig. 14-1.

agent successfully selling manuscripts for her students and many other clients.

There is a large Diamond (No. 3). A most unusual and fantastic combination of lines. Within this Diamond are several stars and smaller Diamonds. This woman has the ability to inspire writers to create material which should prove outstanding. The smaller Diamonds indicate that some of these writers will be financially successful.

The Career Line (No. 4) starts at the base of the little finger, touching the Marriage Line (No. 5) showing that her personal career did not start until after marriage.

There is also a Second Career Line (No. 6). This connects with the Life Line in the center of the base of the palm. Then these combined lines have several strong branches (No. 7) culminating in a perfect Diamond. This woman, in her sixties, is now entering the most creative, active, productive and financially successful period of her life.

The fact that her own Career Line is part of the Diamond (which always indicates security) shows that it comes through her own efforts.

The Fate Line (No. 8) originates under the second finger, the Finger of Finances, then continues downward becoming a part of the largest Diamond, showing that this woman is actually following the blueprint of her fate or destiny.

There is a Square (No. 9) on the Life Line, showing early restrictions. She is an only child with strong parental domination.

The peculiar finger print (No. 10) in the Marriage Sector, between the third and little finger, reveals the health of husband. He is a diabetic.

The fingers are well balanced, round-tipped, showing ability to do detail work which requires concentration. The little finger stands away from the others, when hand is relaxed . . . a strong desire for independence.

The thumb is low set, firm, and blunt. She is outspoken and firm in her decisions.

Altogether, this imprint shows vividly the character of a woman who has not allowed earlier restrictions, disappointments and responsibilities to stand in the way of achieving progress and success in a purposeful way. Not the easy way, but with lots of will power and hard work.

Analysis of Fig. 14-2, the Imprint of an 89 Year Old Lady:

This imprint is dominated by the large Triangle (No. 1). It has its origin on the Heart Line, underneath the little finger, covering the center of the palm. This woman's husband left her and several small children for another woman. Naturally this changed and influenced her entire life.

There are several squares (No. 2). Squares placed in this position show the shouldering of great responsibilities throughout her lifetime.

The upper branch of the Head Line (No. 3), which is also part of the Triangle, connects with the Heart Line, near the Marriage Center, under the little finger. Determination plus good common sense made it possible for her to overcome this experience.

The Head Line curves downward, with several pronounced branches meaning imagination (No. 4). Expression of this imagination is thwarted by the Square (No. 5) over the Fate Line, responsibilities have been placed on her, even in her eighties.

The Heart Line, with its large cross (No. 6) and the cross under the first finger (No. 7) indicates the "Crosses are losses." She has lost several grown children as well as her second husband. See Cross under little finger (No. 8).

There has been much travel; see lines between Life Line and base of thumb.

At 89 this grand lady is physically active, mentally alert and is a living example of a tremendous ability to overcome obstacles.

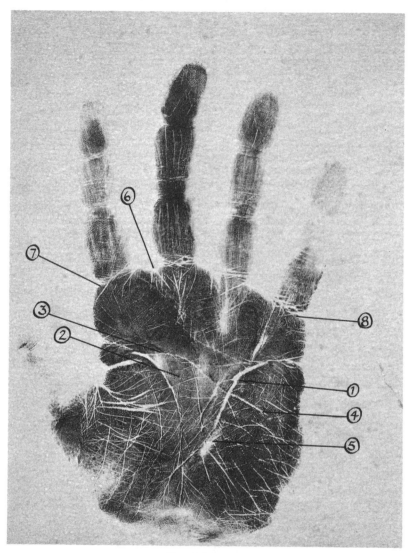

Fig. 14-2.

Analysis of Fig. 14-3

This imprint is unusual because it is completely uncomplicated and the Lines are deep, well formed, and unbroken.

The Head Line (No. 1) is exceptionally straight, showing a practical mind, untroubled by tension or worries. It is joined to the Life Line, a further indication that "down-to-earthness" and common sense rule the life of this individual.

There is a Diamond between the second and third fingers, showing early establishment of security, with this woman contributing to that security. (2)

The Heart Line turns toward the first finger (No. 3). It has many small lines beneath it, but not touching the Heart Line. This shows friendliness, the ability to meet people and one whose emotions are controlled by the straight, strong Head Line.

The family lines (No. 4) clearly indicate the five children in her family. Two brothers and three girls.

There is a large cross, beneath these lines (No. 5), indicating the loss of a parent (father) at an early age.

Another large cross (No. 6) in the center of the palm (not touching any line) shows the sudden, shocking death of her sister in her early forties.

The Palm is Square. A capable hand. The wide spread between thumb and first finger indicates a love of people.

The little finger is extended, away from the others, when hand is relaxed. Desire for personal independence is shown.

The absence of a Fate Line indicates that this individual's life should not be changed through unexpected events over which she has no control.

Analysis of Fig. 14-4: (A Four Year Old Girl)

This hand imprint is important because of the depth and clarity of the major lines. The minor, or emotional lines have not developed. There is little likelihood that too many of these will

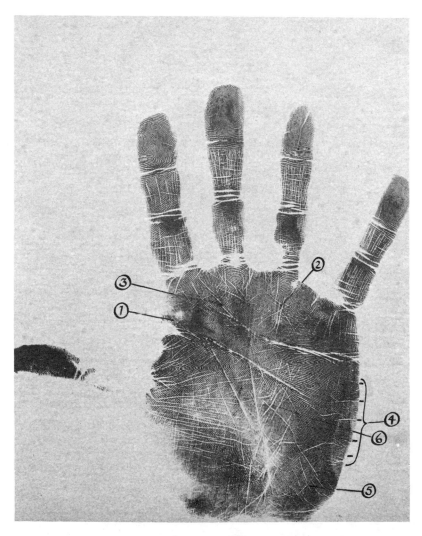

Fig. 14-3.

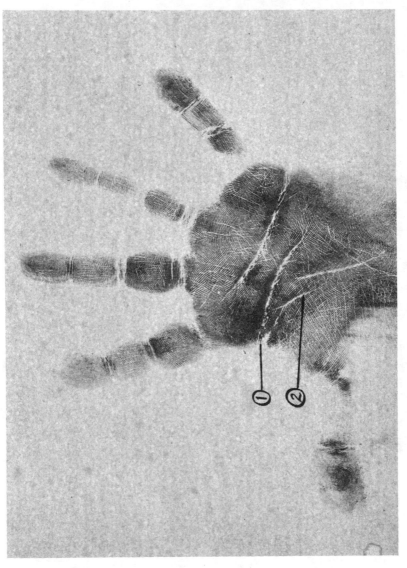

Fig. 14-4.

appear, as the Head Line (No. 1) is strong and clear. Reason should certainly be a ruling factor in her life.

The Heart Line (No. 2) is also strong and well balanced.

The Life Line, in the left hand (No. 1) is connected to the Head Line. Further indication that she will reason things out and not act on impulse.

There is a well defined Diamond at the end of the Life Line. She should have better than average security through most of her life.

The Life Line in the right hand (No. 2) has a decided break, with a fine line connecting it to the line in the center of palm. In most instances this indicates a drastic change in a woman's life through marriage.

The thumbs are extremely low set. A very friendly, out-going child. She should develop intellectually to a high degree, although there is not too much evidence of an individual career.

Study the hand of the 89 year old Lady and then examine this 4 year old girl's imprint. You will find it most interesting and educational, as the years do add lines to the hand, as one goes through emotional experiences. However, the major lines seldom show any pronounced changes.

CONCLUSION

We have given you, in the preceding chapters, our conception of Hand Analysis, gained through many years of practical experience and the study of thousands of hands.

We have been quite revolutionary in many instances, completely overthrowing the old traditions. We fully believe that we have been right in so doing, because our research has proven conclusively that many of the "Superstitions and Suppositions" of another day have no place in modern Hand Analysis. Every theory, idea and opinion, no matter what it may be, is subject to change, or else we would still believe the world is flat.

In this book, we have tried to make every detail as clear as possible in order to give you a definite working knowledge of the fascinating study of Hand Analysis.

A book on any subject can only lay down the rules as fundamentals. Such is the case here. Your proficiency in actual practice depends upon your patience, research and study. The more time you spend in these activities, the more progress you will make.

We have stressed many times in this book that you cannot take one, two or three indications and complete the whole story of the hand, or arrive at a definite understanding of character or condition. You must balance many contradictory evidences. This is called Synthesis.

In synthesizing a hand, you blend all the important factors into one picture. This can be compared to building up a jig-saw puzzle. You take a piece here, another there, fit these together and then others begin to automatically drop in place, until at last that which was a confused mass of individual and disjointed parts becomes a distinct and readable whole.

There is another factor in Hand Analysis which is important . . . the "Sense of Analysis." This attribute is hard to describe . . . call it Hunch, Intuition, "sensory perception" . . . or anything you like. But no matter what you label this peculiar "something" it will always work in the same way . . . enabling you to arrive at very quick, definite conclusions. It is the instinctive sensing of something about the person with whom you may be in conference, which brings out many things that do not show in the hand to a beginner. Whenever you have one of these peculiar impressions, do not hesitate to mention it, no matter how farfetched it may appear to you. If you do this, you will be surprised at the accuracy.

"Sense of Analysis" goes hand in glove with "Synthesis." In synthesizing a hand . . . seeing groupings of lines, marks, etc., which at first appear to be quite contradictory, this "Analytical Sense," will often flash out, giving you the ability to give an immediate and correct interpretation.

Some persons will have more "Analytical Sense" than others. Just as some individuals instinctively understand and appreciate music. But all have it to a certain degree. It only needs practical expression to develop.

Again this reminder in the final closing. Hand Analysis can and should be used in a most constructive and helpful manner. Do not start out with an idea of finding only the negative aspect. We have sincerely attempted to give you the higher, more helpful side. We hope you will bear with us in your developement and practice.

Whether you use Hand Analysis as a profession, or merely as a pastime . . . keep it on a high plane. Never drag it down into the dregs of "negativism" and become an alarmist in your interpretations.

There is an ancient Oriental saying: "He who uses knowledge for destructive purposes . . . that knowledge will destroy." It is a pretty good thing to remember, but a better thing to do: To work with the construction gang and not with the wrecking crew.